CELEBRATION
of
A•M•E•R•I•C•A•N
FOOD

Sailing off in search of spices, Columbus discovered the New World, a veritable cornucopia of native foods. Currants, pictured here in an 1869 lithograph by L. Prang & Co. based on a painting by Virginia Granbery, were one of the many kinds of fruit found growing wild.

CELEBRATION

of

A·M·E·R·I·C·A·N

FOOD

Four Centuries in the Melting Pot

Gerry Schremp

Fulcrum Publishing
Golden, Colorado

Published in cooperation with the Library of Congress

Edd and Carrie Severt peel potatoes for lunch in their farmhouse kitchen in Allegheny County, North Carolina. Photo by Lyntha Scott Eiler, 1978.

Photo research by Diane Hamilton

Library of Congress Cataloging-in-Publication Data

Schremp, Geraldine.
 Celebration of American food : four centuries in the melting pot / Gerry Schremp.
  p.   cm.
 Includes bibliographical references and index.
 ISBN 1-55591-226-5 (hardcover : alk. paper)
 1. Diet—United States—History. 2. Food habits—United States—History. 3. Cookery—United States—History. I. Title.
 TX360.U6S37 1996
 394.1'0973—dc20   95–35783
                                                            CIP

Printed by Sung In Printing Company in Seoul, Korea
0 9 8 7 6 5 4 3 2 1

Fulcrum Publishing
350 Indiana Street, Suite 350
Golden, Colorado 80401-5093
(800) 992-2908 • (303) 277-1623

Contents

Flavored carbonated water first appeared around 1830. The public quickly embraced this sugared refreshment, called "an American drink" by *Harper's Weekly*. Early flavors included birch beer, pepsin, ginger, kola and cherry, as shown in this 1897 ad art lithographed by Ketterlinus.

A celebration of the Pilgrims' first harvest in 1621, Thanksgiving became a national holiday in 1863, when President Abraham Lincoln declared the last Thursday in November as the official day. Illustration by Edward Penfield published as cover of *Collier's*, November 25, 1901.

Foreword

*T*his volume, the eighth in the Library of Congress Classics series of illustrated books, celebrates an essential ingredient in the history of our country—food. A bountiful nation, the United States has long been particularly rich in its variety of plants and animals. And, as Gerry Schremp makes clear in her lively text, the American people have created, from these elements, an ever-evolving culinary life and a distinctive culinary heritage spiced with the traditions of many cultures.

In *Celebration of American Food,* Ms. Schremp describes how the history of American food is inextricably bound up with the history of America itself, from the earliest European settlers' education in the diet of indigenous people (and the subsequent enrichment of European tables when indigenous American plants and recipes were exported) to the advertising of food and the mechanization of the kitchen in our own era. She tells us of times when depression or war diminished America's bounty, and how American cooks adapted, creating new dishes with what was at hand. She considers regional dishes, supermarkets, food fads and manias and the kitchens where culinary history was made in this sweeping and informative overview. And, delightfully, she adds zest to the mix by including recipes—making this a volume that provides not only cogent observations and food for thought, but actual tastes of our culinary history.

The illustrations in this volume also provide tastes, albeit figurative ones, of the many ways in which the history of food—particularly American food—is celebrated in the collections of the Library of Congress, now comprising some 110 million items. From many thousands of cookbooks, to periodicals, commercial and fine art, and motion pictures, to music and maps, the Library provides a feast for researchers interested in American culinary history.

We collect this material as part of our mandate to preserve American history and culture. But the history of the Library—which in the year 2000 will celebrate the 200th anniversary of its founding—makes it especially fitting that the history of American food is so amply represented in our collections. The Library's principal founder, Thomas Jefferson, was both a student of history and a man who appreciated fine foods. A farmer, he experimented with new crops and with crop rotation. A collector of recipes, he was the first president to enjoy ice cream in the White House—the dessert made from a recipe he brought back from Europe. A scientist and inventor, he drew plans for many helpful domestic devices—including a macaroni maker. That plan is part of the Library's collections.

About a century ago, Oliver Wendell Holmes said, "The true essentials of a feast are only fun and feed." You will find those true essentials in this *Celebration of American Food*. We are pleased to cooperate with Fulcrum Publishing in presenting it to you.

—James H. Billington
The Librarian of Congress

To smoke fish for winter storage, Native Americans constructed a platform made of stakes and built a fire beneath it. Seafood, both fish and shellfish, was an important food source for coastal tribes.

Introduction

This series of illustrations from an early book by Fray Bernadino de Florentine demonstrates the importance of corn (maize) in the Native American diet.

*L*ong before America became famous for Coca-Cola and McDonald's hamburgers, Spanish Conquistadores were introducing the world to foods indigenous to the Western Hemisphere. That much-quoted nineteenth century French gourmet Anthelme Brillat-Savarin called the turkey "one of the New World's finest gifts to the Old." His gratitude rightfully goes to the remarkable peoples dubbed American Indians who had domesticated that bird—along with more than 150 plants ranging from vegetables to tobacco, dyes to medicines.

Although often called "Native Americans," the Indians are, in fact, the first immigrants. They are descendants of nomadic Asian hunters who trudged from Siberia to Alaska across the Bering Strait, which was dry land during an Ice Age eons ago when most of the world's water was locked up in glaciers. The hunters came, a family or a clan at a time, over thousands of years, beginning about 15,000 B.C. according to some experts—about 30,000 B.C. say others.

The game they sought most avidly were herds of such creatures as mastodons, woolly mammoths and giant beavers as big as bears. While the men hunted, the women and children gathered berries, nuts, herbs, roots and wood for fires to roast the meat.

During temporary periods of warm weather when the ice sheets covering the land melted partially, passages formed so that hunters could travel south and eastward. By the time the glaciers retreated between 10,000 and 8,000 B.C., and the Bering Strait land bridge was submerged under water hundreds of feet deep, Indians had reached Tierra del Fuego.

Dispersed throughout the Americas, the Indians developed hundreds of cultures, each speaking its own dialect and worshipping its own gods. Giant animals became extinct, but many North American peoples remained itinerant, following bison, deer, moose, elk and small game that roamed woodlands and prairies. The ice melt expanded breeding grounds in the far north, leading to increases in flocks of migrating birds. Schools of fish spawning in rivers and lakes created by glaciers made fishing more productive. Wild plant foods still were prized, however, and Indians often timed migrations to coincide with the ripening of fruit as well as the movements of herds.

Some Indians, particularly in Central America and western South America, settled down to nurture native plants: tomatoes, potatoes, bell peppers, chilies, chayotes, peanuts, pineapples, papayas, avocados, cherimoyas, cocoa and vanilla among others. Archaeologists have found that peppers, beans and squashes were cultivated about 7,000 B.C. The oldest traces of corn date to 4,000 B.C.

Over millennia, food crops were carried north and south. Wherever Indians farmed, odds are they planted corn. It could be adapted to most climates; its seeds were easily stored and carried. Ears could be boiled or roasted and the kernels eaten green; dried kernels could be ground into meal or boiled with wood ash and water (lye) to remove the tough skins and produce tender hominy that might be dried for boiling whole at a later date or grinding to grits. Corn was almost always grown and eaten with beans and squash. The Iroquois called them "The Three Sisters."

Indian farmers rang a host of changes on their crops. By the time of Columbus, they had developed dozens of types of corn; it grew in a rainbow of hues—white, yellow, red, purple, blue, black and variegated—and in lengths up to 18 inches. Besides edible podded green and wax beans, Indians had lima beans and "common" or kidney beans—speckled or plain black, red, pink, yellow, green or brown.

To supplement their diet, Indians gathered honey and collected maple sap, which they boiled down into syrup and sugar. They reaped wild rice and harvested wild fruit: North America alone yielded twenty kinds of blueberries and a dozen kinds of gooseberries, plus currants, strawberries and elderberries. There were grapes, plums and persimmons as well.

Early explorers were amazed by the variety of Indian foods. As early as A.D. 1006, Icelandic sagas extolled corn. Norsemen found grapes so abundant that they named their landfall Vinland. Although Columbus didn't find the Spice Islands, he returned to Spain in 1492 with corn, and in 1493 he returned with sweet potatoes and chilies—"pepper more pungent than that from the Caucasus," according to a contemporary. Cortés brought back tomatoes and cocoa from Mexico, and Pizarro returned from Peru with white potatoes.

During the sixteenth century, America's culinary treasury was opened to Europe, Africa and Asia. Some foods, like turkey and pepper, met with instant success. Others were treated warily. The tomato, for example, was eaten in Italy by 1550, but the plant belongs to the deadly nightshade family so that many Europeans once thought it poisonous.

Today Indian crops have been refined and hybridized. The corn is sweeter, the peppers plumper and the tomatoes smoother. And diners everywhere savor the Indians' bounty. Italy's polenta (corn), Spain's gazpacho (tomatoes), Austria's Sacher Torte (chocolate), Mozambique's chicken-groundnut stew (peanuts), China's Szechuan lamb (hot chilies) and France's cassoulet (beans)—are all foods first enjoyed in the New World.

Plains Indians followed migrating bison herds, hunting the animals for their meat, as in this 1837 lithograph by E.C. Biddle, and also utilizing the fur, bones and hides to make clothing, tools and shelter.

The Indian "Graine"

The first Englishman to write about corn was Thomas Hariot, who visited Sir Walter Raleigh's ill-fated colony on Roanoke Island, and published A Briefe & True Report of the New Found Land in Virginia in 1588. He rhapsodized that corn, which he called pagatowr, produced "a very white and sweete floure … (that) maketh a very good bread." And he was astonished by the sophistication of Indian agriculture. He reported that the farmers timed their planting so they could harvest three crops a year of this "graine of marvelous increase." Taken together, these crops yielded 200 bushels an acre whereas in England "fourtie bushelles of our wheate … is thought to be much."

Chapter One
Americanizing European Cookery (1607-1775)

*W*herever they came from—England, Holland, Germany, Sweden—the first European settlers in America had to change the way they ate and drank. Most fruits and vegetables that Indians offered were strange; animals, birds and fish belonged to unfamiliar species. Imposing a traditional seventeenth century menu on corn, pumpkin and turkey taxed a cook's imagination, although it apparently did not dim his enthusiasm.

"Heaven and earth never agreed better to frame a place for man's habitation," wrote Captain John Smith about the Virginia plantation. Flights of birds nearly blotted out the sky; oysters lay "thick as stones" on beaches and there were "fine and beautiful Strawberries, foure times bigger and better than ours in England."

Despite nature's generosity, few Englishmen who settled at Jamestown, Virginia, in May 1607, survived. The water got brackish. Huge flocks of birds migrated south. Berries were seasonal. Deer and turkey left as the leaves fell. Shellfish seemed to disappear in winter.

Friendly Algonquins gave the English food and lessons in how to plant corn, but most newcomers were Cavaliers—aristocrats—with no experience at living off the land, much less growing crops, and no desire to learn. They intended to find gold and get rich quick. Instead, they died. Their supplies ran out; they battled Indians; they were felled by disease. When ships returned the next year, just thirty-eight of the 105 men remained alive. Still, recruits arrived each spring. By 1609, Jamestown's population had reached five hundred. That winter proved disastrous; only sixty lived through the "Starving Time."

In a 1920 painting by Clyde O. Deland entitled *The Beginning of New England,* early settlers build a home in the wilderness. When the *Mayflower* landed in 1620, the Pilgrims were ill-prepared for life in the New World. Indians showed them how to plant corn, catch fish, trap small game and gather fruit and nuts.

Gradually, however, the colonists turned wilderness into farms. In 1612, they exported tobacco as a cash crop. By 1630 they numbered about twenty-five hundred, well-housed and well-fed. They had cattle, goats and swine in abundance, "plentie" bread and "good ale, both strong and small."

Founding New England

The Pilgrim families left England in September 1620 aboard the *Mayflower* bound for Hudson's River, but the ship was blown north to Cape Cod. In mid-November they anchored in the relative safety of the place "which in Captain Smith's map is called Plimouth."

According to the Pilgrims' governor, William Bradford, "they found diverse cornfields and little running brooks, a place fit for situation" when they landed December 11, 1620. However, Bradford proved as overly optimistic as Smith. The Pilgrims were poorly provisioned and most were townspeople unprepared for a wilderness. That bleak winter, they ate acorns, mussels, roots and potherbs. Almost half of the Pilgrims died.

With spring arrived Squanto, a Wampanoag Indian who brought hope. Squanto had been taken to Europe as a slave in 1614 and learned English. When he made his way back to Massachusetts, his village of Patuxet on the site of Plymouth had been wiped out by smallpox. The lonely Squanto welcomed the Pilgrims and helped them make peace with the local Indian chief, Massasoit. Squanto showed the Pilgrims how to weave vines into nets to catch fish, how to tramp eels from the muddy shore and how to trap rabbits. He introduced them to cranberries and black walnuts.

Most important, Squanto taught them to plant corn in mounds several feet apart, tucking beans in with the kernels and setting three herring, arranged so the noses met, on top as fertilizer. Squash was planted between mounds. As they grew, corn stalks supported bean vines, and squash leaves helped keep out weeds. After harvest, corn, beans and squash were cooked in a mixture still known by its Indian name *succotash*.

Indian Pudding

Cornmeal puddings were the first kind early settlers could cook. This spicy version resembles gingerbread.

> 1/2 cup cornmeal
> 4-1/2 cups milk
> 2 eggs
> 1 cup molasses
> 1/2 teaspoon ground cinnamon
> 1/2 teaspoon ground ginger

Mix cornmeal with 4 cups of the milk in the top of a double boiler. Set over gently boiling water and whisk until smooth. Cover and cook over low heat for about 20 minutes. Meanwhile, in a small bowl, lightly beat eggs. Stir in molasses, cinnamon and ginger. Remove the cornmeal from the heat and blend in the egg mixture. Ladle into a buttered 2-quart baking dish and pour 1/2 cup milk over the top. Bake at 350°F for 1 hour. Serve with whipped cream, if desired. Serves 6 to 8.

Counting Corn

When the Puritans planted corn, they put enough kernels into each hillock to guarantee at least one sprout. Some favored arranging four kernels in a circle; others inserted six or seven kernels. Centuries later the children of Massachusetts could still chant a rhyme Pilgrims may have repeated as they worked:

> One for the cutworm
> One for the crow
> Two to perish
> And three to grow.

The Pilgrims also planted wheat and barley seeds from England. These failed, but the harvest of Indian foods was so gratifying that they declared a holiday and invited the Indians to the feast. Chief Massasoit arrived with about ninety braves and four deer to supplement the Pilgrims' bounty.

Settling in

Over the years, the Pilgrims carved farms and villages out of the rocky wilderness. Livestock arrived. Later, settlers brought cuttings of European fruit trees; these grew so well that apple pie became the epitome of Americanism. Maple trees were tapped for their sugary sap. European bees imported in the 1630s gave cooks a choice of "tree sweetenin'" or "bee sweetenin'."

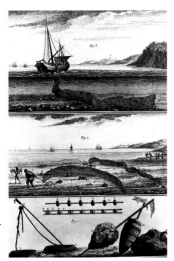

As indicated in these eighteenth-century engravings from *Traite General des Pesches* by Duhamel du Monceau, the waters were teeming with fish, of which cod was the most abundant—hence the name Cape Cod.

The colonists mastered the sea: fish were "Pilgrims' bread," and dried cod was known as "Cape Cod turkey." Shellfish abounded, oysters grew 6 inches long and lobsters grew to 6 pounds.

Similarly, colonists became marksmen and kept family stewpans full with venison, hare, rabbit and squirrel. Bear meat was considered delicious, and produced precious fat. Waterfowl blanketed fields during migration. Flocks of passenger pigeons darkened the sky. Year-round, the hunter found fowl and trapped turkey flocks of a hundred or more in wood corrals.

New colonists arrived annually. By 1640, Massachusetts had a population of twenty-one thousand in thirty-nine settlements. Settlers dispersed north into what is now New Hampshire and Vermont, and south into Connecticut and Rhode Island.

Men and women stack cleaned fish on the beach in another engraving from *Traite General des Pesches*.

The Dutch established New Amsterdam at the mouth of the Hudson River and took over New Sweden on the Delaware River. When the English conquered the Dutch, they renamed the Hudson River colony New York. English Catholics founded Maryland; Virginians settled North Carolina and English settled South Carolina. English Quakers went to Pennsylvania, followed by Germans or *Deutsch* (Pennsylvania Dutch). After 1733, Georgia was a buffer against the French to the west and the Spanish to the south.

The Growth of Wealth

Whether they came for God or gain, most colonists considered themselves English. They were loyal to the king though they chafed at rules and taxes imposed on them.

Nine out of ten people lived on farms. Fields and orchards supplied grain, vegetables and fruits. Poultry produced eggs, cows and goats gave milk and meat, sheep furnished mutton and wool and pigs yielded hams and lard. Ponds and streams supplied fish. All the "boughten" foods required were salt, spices, molasses, sugar, rum, whiskey and beer. (Water was often polluted and milk was only for babies. Alcoholic drinks—the stronger, the better—were vital. Even children used them to quench thirst caused by a diet of salty food.)

Colonial villages were small—maybe only a store and a few houses at a crossroads or a port on the ocean or a river. By the time of the Revolution, just a few towns had a population of ten thousand or more, yet wealth accumulated. Exporting tobacco and indigo enriched some southern plantation owners. So did rice,

Early Brewing

The first brewery in America was established at the tip of Manhattan by Dutch settlers in 1612. When the English took control and the island became New York, there were four beer taverns. The beverage's basic ingredient was malted grain—corn, barley, oats or wheat—flavored with anything from pumpkins to Jerusalem artichokes, from persimmons to spruce bark. To make the beer palatable and acceptably potent, it was sweetened with molasses and spiked with rum.

introduced to South Carolina with seed from Madagascar in the 1680s and 1690s. By 1700, rice was called "Carolina gold."

With forests standing almost at the water's edge, New England shipbuilders and sea captains prospered. During the English Civil Wars from 1640 to 1660, American shipping expanded into the West Indies, trading lumber and fish for molasses. (In 1494, Columbus introduced sugar cane to the Caribbean; by 1512 African slaves were working cane fields.)

In New England, molasses was distilled into rum. Boston alone produced over one million gallons in 1731. Some rum went tò the profitable, if dangerous, triangular trade: molasses to New England, rum to Africa, slaves to the Caribbean.

Colonial Menus

Wherever they settled, colonists attempted to grow familiar crops or, at the least, to concoct European-style dishes with ingredients they found in America. They kept to traditional ways even when bread was made with corn instead of wheat and beer brewed from pumpkins, parsnips and walnut tree chips.

Peas planted early thrived. Carrots and parsnips, introduced at Jamestown, became favorites with Indians as well as colonists. Barley did well and served as the base for both beer and bread. The English brought their strong cravings for meats and sweets with them. The Dutch diet emphasized meats, too, and required copious supplies of lard. Both demanded dairy products.

The Pilgrims were grateful for having survived their first year in the new country and invited Indians to feast with them. The celebration depicted in *The First Thanksgiving at Plymouth* by L.G. Ferris lasted three days and included venison, duck, goose, shellfish, smoked eels, corn bread, leeks, watercress, plums, berries and wine made from wild grapes. Whether turkey was actually served at the first Thanksgiving is undocumented.

Syllabub

In their heyday, syllabubs were thought very classy and were often served at fancy balls.

> 1/2 cup white wine or sherry
> 2 tablespoons brandy
> 2 tablespoons lemon juice
> 2 teaspoons grated lemon peel
> 1-1/2 cups heavy cream
> 1/3 cup sugar

Combine white wine or sherry with brandy, lemon juice and lemon peel. Chill overnight. Whip cream until it forms soft peaks. Sprinkle sugar over the cream and whip until the peaks are firm. Gently blend the wine mixture into the cream. Serve from tall goblets, grating nutmeg on top if desired. Serves 6 to 8.

Codfish Cakes

1 pound salt cod	1 tablespoon chopped parsley
4–5 cups diced white potatoes	1 teaspoon dry mustard
1/4 cup milk	pepper
2 eggs	1 cup fine bread crumbs (if desired)

Soak salt cod for at least 12 hours in several changes of water. Drain cod, dice it and boil in fresh water with potatoes for 15 minutes or until fish flakes and potatoes are tender. Drain. Mash together until smooth, beat in milk, eggs, parsley, dry mustard and a grating of pepper. Taste for seasoning. Shape into a dozen flat cakes. Coat with bread crumbs, if desired. Fry in 1-inch-deep fat for about 3 minutes on each side until golden brown. Serves 6. Codfish cakes are often accompanied by tomato sauce.

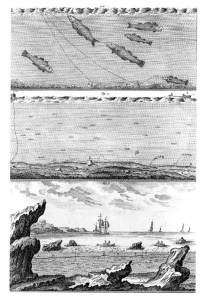

Cod fishing [Newfoundland?]. Engraving in Traite General des Pesches, 1769, by Duhamel du Monceau. Besides cod, other harvests from the sea included flounder, sole, herring, halibut, sturgeon, smelt and drum along with lobster, oysters, clams and other shellfish. The fishing industry thrived, exporting goods back to Europe. By the end of the seventeenth century, fishing was the main industry of Massachusetts Bay.

During the colonial years (and along the frontiers for almost three centuries) game replaced farm animals. Soups, hashes and stews were made with turkey and venison instead of chicken or beef. Southerners adapted an Indian recipe for squirrel meat and corn, and called it Brunswick stew.

Corn flour took the place of wheat flour in their fondly remembered puddings. For the "Indian" version, corn flour was mixed with molasses, buttermilk, egg and spices, wrapped in cloth and suspended in the kettle above a stew or soup to cook in its rising steam. (If flavors mixed, so much the better.)

Dried wild berries produced passable raisins for scones and mincemeat. Cornmeal, simmered with milk or water, took the place of wheat or oat porridge. The "sallets" (salads) of the Old World were tossed in the New with herbs from kitchen gardens plus wild ferns, cresses and dandelions.

Red Flannel Hash

4 small cooked or canned beets, diced

2–3 large boiled potatoes

1 pound corned beef, cooked and coarsely chopped

1 onion, finely chopped

pepper

nutmeg

four tablespoons lard or drippings

Combine all ingredients in a bowl. Season to taste with black pepper and nutmeg. If possible, refrigerate the hash for several hours so flavors blend. To cook, melt 4 tablespoons lard or drippings in a large, heavy skillet over medium heat. Add hash, press it flat and cook until the bottom browns—about 20 minutes. Turn the hash. Brown it briefly before sliding it onto a platter. Serves 4.

Johnnycakes

Centuries ago some version of this recipe was made for travelers, who stuffed the cakes in their pockets to eat—cold and unadorned—on their journeys. Hence the name journeycake, or, as Rhode Islanders prefer, johnnycake. Today they are eaten like pancakes.

1 cup yellow cornmeal

1/2 teaspoon salt

1 tablespoon melted butter or drippings

1 cup boiling water

1/4–1/2 cup milk

Mix together cornmeal, salt and drippings. Stir in boiling water. Mix until the batter is smooth. Stir in 1/4 cup milk. If the batter is stiff, add up to 1/4 cup more milk. Warm a griddle or heavy skillet over medium heat. Brush it with melted butter or drippings, then ladle out 1/4 cup batter for each cake. Cook for 2 or 3 minutes on both sides until light brown and crisp. Serve johnnycakes hot with butter and maple syrup.

Preserving Foods

In the North, families set small sheds called springhouses over streams to cool butter and cream in summer, or they lowered jugs into deep wells. Southerners dug caves or built insulated icehouses, and during the winter, they loaded them with ice cut from ponds or lakes.

Hens that stopped laying eggs became Sunday dinner. When cows got too old to milk or pull a wagon, they were slaughtered, usually at the start of winter. Cold weather helped preserve meat, and such timing spared the farmer's stock of hay. Sometimes a carcass was shared with neighbors on a reciprocal basis. Or parts not eaten at once could be "corned" with grains—corns—of coarse salt, or pickled with vinegar or sliced and dried into jerky.

Pork was the most common meat since pigs could find their own food. In Boston, pigs became so numerous that a "hogreve" or pigcatcher was hired in 1636 to round them up. Pigs supplied fat that was "tried out," or rendered, into lard. Every household had a barrel filled with pork preserved in salt and vinegar.

Pork also was salted and smoked—by hanging in the kitchen chimney or a smokehouse—to produce ham and bacon. Scraps filled sausages.

New England fishermen dried their catch on rocks in the sun before salting and packing it or they pickled or smoked it. Berries were sun-dried. So were beans, peas, apples, pears and pumpkins. Dried string beans, called leather britches, and slices of other vegetables plus fruits and herbs were threaded on strings and hung from the rafters. Fruits also might be preserved in rum, or turned into fruit butter, jam or jelly. Corn, cabbage and cucumbers were pickled. Apples and pears were pressed into juices, then fermented for long-lasting alcoholic hard cider. Most milk was churned into butter or preserved as cheese. (Children could work a churn, and buttermilk was useful in cooking.)

Root cellars, dug into a hill or tunnelled under the house deep below the frost line, stored root vegetables: potatoes, onions, carrots, turnips. Cellars kept food from freezing in winter or spoiling from heat in summer. Besides vegetables, they held barrels of cider, crocks of fruit and eggs smeared with fat or wax and packed in straw.

Seasonings disguised the fact that meat or fish had been kept too long, so most colonial housewives grew herb gardens and put up crocks of various chutneys and catsups (usually with bases of fruits like peaches or grapes, or nuts). Some of the best relishes were made by Pennsylvania cooks who served seven sweets and seven sours as side dishes at every meal. These ranged from apple butter to tangy corn relish.

Despite all the work it represented, the stock of winter foods dwindled quickly. Early spring—before the first greens sprouted in the garden—came to be called "the six weeks want."

Cooking Colonial Style

The heart of a colonial home was its kitchen, where food was cooked in the same huge fireplace that the family used to heat the house and light it at night. In the simplest stone-and-mud fireplace, the house-

---

Pease Porridge

Today porridge means cooked cereal, such as oatmeal, but the word derives from the French potage meaning soup, and the colonists used it that way.

2 cups dried split peas	1 celery rib
2 quarts water	1 carrot
1 onion, peeled and stuck with 3 cloves	1 bay leaf

For this porridge, combine all ingredients in a large pot. Bring to a boil, reduce the heat and simmer for 2 hours or until the peas are very soft. Remove and discard the onion, celery, carrot and bay leaf. Taste the porridge and season with salt and black pepper. Serves 4 to 6.

To drefs Haddock the Spanifh Way.

Take two fine haddocks, fcale, gut, and wafh them well, wipe them with a cloth, and broil them; put a pint of fweet oil in a ftew-pan, feafon it with pepper and falt, a little cloves, mace, and nutmeg beaten two cloves of garlick chopped, pare half a dozen love apples and quarter them, when in feafon, put them in, and a fpoonful of vinegar, put in the fifh, and ftew them very gently for half an hour over a flow fire; put them in a hot difh, and garnifh with lemon.

To drefs Haddocks the Jews Way.

Take two fine large haddocks, fcale, gut, and wafh them very clean, cut them in flices three inches thick, and dry them in a cloth; put half a pint of fweet oil in a ftew-pan, a middling onion and a handful of parfley chopped fine, let it boil up, put in the fifh with half a pint of water, feafon it with beaten mace, pep-

Settlers had to adapt to unfamiliar foods, although they attempted to re-create European-style dishes from the ingredients they found in America. This recipe from *The New Art of Cookery,* published in 1792, describes haddock made the Spanish and Jewish ways, with "garlick"—a European herb—as well as "love apples," better known as tomatoes.

The Kitchen Garden, from John Parkinson's *Paradisi in Sole...,* 1756. Herbs were a staple in colonial gardens, as were potatoes, which could be stored in the root cellar through the cold winter months.

Baked Beans

4 cups dried peas or Great Northern beans	2 teaspoons dry mustard
1 onion stuck with 3 whole cloves	1 teaspoon black pepper
1 cup molasses	2 cups water
1 tablespoon vinegar	1/2 pound lean salt pork

Soak beans in water and cover overnight. Drain. Place the onion, stuck with cloves, in a 2-1/2 to 3-quart bean pot or casserole. Add the beans. Stir in molasses, vinegar, mustard, pepper and water. Cut salt pork into 4 pieces and slash into the rind; tuck the pork under the beans. Cover the pot tightly and bake at 250°F for 8 hours or overnight, until the beans are tender. Taste and season. Serves 6 to 8.

Fish House Punch

This punch was invented about 1732 by members of the Philadelphia's Colony of the State in Schuylkill Fishing Club, the oldest eating club in America. (After the Revolution, the name was changed to the State in Schuylkill Fishing Club.)

> 1-1/2 cups sugar
> 4 cups water
> 2 cups strained fresh lemon juice
> 1 bottle brandy
> 2 bottles rum
> 2 cups peach brandy

Dissolve sugar in water and add fresh lemon juice. Pour in brandy, rum and peach brandy. Chill for at least 6 hours. Put a large piece of ice in a punch bowl and pour the brandy mixture over it. Makes about 4 quarts.

Pound Cake

The earliest printed mention of this cake in the colonies was in 1747. The basic recipe—like this one—calls for a pound each of butter, sugar and flour, plus eggs. Traditional flavorings include rum, brandy, bourbon, orange juice and vanilla; some cakes contained caraway seeds or citron.

2 cups butter	2 teaspoons vanilla
2 cups sugar	4 cups flour
8 eggs, separated	1 teaspoon cream of tartar
1 tablespoon rum	

Cream together butter and sugar until fluffy. Beat in egg yolks, one at a time. Flavor with rum and vanilla extract. Sift flour gradually into the batter. Beat egg whites with cream of tartar until they form stiff peaks. Fold them into the batter. Turn the batter into two buttered and floured 9-by-5-inch loaf pans. Bake at 325°F for 1 hour or until the cakes spring back when pressed lightly. Let the cakes cool on racks for 15 minutes before removing them from the pans.

wife hung her kettle of soup or stew by a chain or hook from a lug pole anchored above the fire. The pole was green wood to resist fire; even so it might burn through, dumping dinner and scalding the cook.

When the stone fireplace gave way to one of bricks and mortar, the lug pole was replaced by a swinging iron crane—an American innovation—provided with hooks of various lengths so a pot could be moved up or down to make its contents boil or gently simmer. The crane swung outward so a cook could check dinner without ducking into the fireplace.

As colonists discovered deposits of iron ore and developed ironworks, kettles and pots increased in variety. A spider—a skillet on three long legs that stood in the fire—was used for frying. Baking was done in a Dutch oven—a long-legged kettle that had a rimmed lid to hold coals.

Later an oven was built into the side of a fireplace; a fire was burned in it to heat the bricks, then the ashes were swept out and food was pushed in with a wood peel. Beans and breads, which needed lengthy baking, went in first. Cakes went last so they could be taken out early. The oven was closed with a wood, later iron, door.

In the South, where summers were stifling, the kitchen was a separate building or group of buildings. This kept the main house cool and odor-free and lessened the danger of its going up in flames. Even up North, the kitchen was often separated from the house by a porch or gallery. Anywhere, open fires were dangerous: long skirts and sleeves had to be held back lest they ignite.

Eating Etiquette

Except on Sunday, which was a day of prayer and rest, family members were generally too busy to eat together. Anyone who was hungry took a portion from the stew in the kettle (and probably ate standing up because chairs were rare). On Sunday, all the food was put on the table at one time. Everybody in the whole family helped themselves with fingers or homemade spoons. Eating was messy so colonists tied huge napkins around their necks.

Most families ate from trenchers, slabs of wood scooped out on one side, the parents sharing one trencher and the children another. (A young woman and man announced their engagement by sharing a trencher.) After the main course,

the trencher was turned over and dessert was served on the clean wood. According to historian Gerard Carson, "Upcountry, they spoke of the dinner side and the pie side." Some families dispensed with trenchers, serving "spoon meat" on thick slices of bread that soaked up juices and could be eaten, too.

Often entire families shared one wood or pewter mug or noggin. There were few knives; spoons were fashioned from gourds, horns or shells. Forks were newfangled, even in England. (In 1633, Governor John Winthrop became the first Plymouth settler to acquire one.)

As the colonies prospered, tableware and table manners improved in the original settlements—if not on the frontier. By the mid-1700s wealthy families had separate dining rooms with cloth-covered tables, fine chairs and china and pewter (at times silver) to replace woodenware. A fork, knife and spoon were set by every place.

The food got better along with the table settings. Many families ate three times a day—breakfast at sunrise, a full dinner at noontime and a late light supper, consisting mainly of dinner's leftovers. A traveler to Virginia in 1746 reported to the *London Magazine*: "All over the colony ... full tables ... speak somewhat like the old Roast-beef Ages of our Forefathers. Their Breakfast Tables have ... Coffee, Tea, Chocolate, Venison-pasty, Punch, and Beer, or Cyder ... their Dinner, good Beef, Veal, Mutton, Venison, Turkies and Geese, wild and tame, Fowls ... Pies, Puddings ... ."

In addition to crops that settlers learned about from local Indians, other "native American" foods found their way to the colonies by way of Europe. Cortés drank Aztec *cacahuatl* ("gift from the gods") in Mexico and returned to Spain with cacao beans. The first, and now legendary, North American chocolate factory—financed by Walter Baker's grandfather—opened in Dorchester, Massachusetts, in 1765 using West Indian beans.

The kitchen was the largest room in the house, and the fireplace was the center of the kitchen, where the housewife cooked over a wood fire in cast-iron kettles. As a Savannah, Georgia, home built in 1818 shows, brick ovens built into the wall next to the fireplace were used for baking.

Chapter Two
Creating Regional Variations on a Theme (1775–1860)

*T*he thirteen colonies that had clung to the Atlantic coast before the Revolutionary War saw their inhabitants pour west across the Appalachians after the war had ended. Americans joined immigrants, most of whom came from Ireland or Germany, to claim what seemed an inexhaustible supply of virgin land. Each generation traveled farther—from Vermont, perhaps, to New York, then Ohio and finally Wisconsin. The nation's territory ballooned from 350,000 square miles in 1790 to more than 1,835,000 by 1860; its population soared from three million to above thirty million. Trading posts spawned villages that became towns, and towns turned into cities. Business and industry spurred the growth of cities, especially in the northeast.

As the nation grew, the variety in its climates, terrains and citizenry gave each region special character. Political differences eventually led to the Civil War; food differences led to distinctive regional cookery although the nation's English heritage was still evident, particularly among wealthy city dwellers and plantation owners who could import European foods.

Pickled buffalo tongue was considered a delicacy in fancy New York restaurants, and the animals were hunted en masse to supply well-heeled diners. Often only the buffaloes' tongues were cut out, the carcasses left to rot on the plains. *Scott's Bluff's*, an engraving by C. Fenn in *Route from Liverpool to Great Salt Lake Valley*, 1855, by Frederick Hawkins Piercy.

New England Cooking

By the time of the Revolution, game was getting scarce in New England, but livestock guaranteed that the working man's menu would include meat at least once a day. Rib-sticking stews and boiled dinners of meat and vegetables found favor; so did the Pilgrims' baked beans with Boston brown bread. Desserts were rich and traditional: thick custard, creamy syllabub, flummery, raisin-filled pudding and mince pie.

The rivers and streams flowed with fish. In spring, shad arrived by the millions; one man reported over five thousand in a single haul of the net. The ocean brought dozens of kinds of fish as well as shellfish.

Oysters were taken in gigantic quantities and peddled from barrows in coastal cities. The rich drank champagne with oysters; the poor drank beer. Both enjoyed them so much that oysters developed into a national craze. The "Oyster Express," a wagon loaded with live oysters layered in straw

The cover to "The Supper Bell Polka, circa 1858," signifies the growing emphasis on elegant dining. Dinner parties might have eight to ten courses, with a different wine for each course. There was a new formality, and in well-to-do homes the dining room was now separate from the kitchen.

The eating habits of the colonists changed as they adapted to a new country, yet European traditions remained strong, especially for English favorites, such as plum pudding—like the one being served in this 1858 lithograph.

An autumn event, the apple bee was a festive time to gather with neighbors for communal chores. In addition to peeling and slicing apples for drying, there was dancing and eating and drinking hard cider, the most commonly consumed beverage in colonial New England. Wood engraving in *Harper's Weekly,* November 26, 1859.

Labeled *Life Preserver*, this 1856 cookbook was probably indispensable to German immigrants just arriving in the United States. The first American cookbook appeared in 1796, although it featured mostly English recipes. Later cookbooks reflected regional "Americanized" cooking, such as Philomelia Harden's 1842 book entitled *Everybody's Cook and Receipt Book: But More Particularly Designed for Buckeyes, Hoosiers, Wolverines, Corncrackers, Suckers, and All Epicures Who Wish to Live with the Present Times.*

kept wet with salt water, carried them from Baltimore to Cincinnati in the 1820s. During winters in the late 1830s, oysters were transported by sleigh to Chicago; by the 1850s, railroads carried ice-packed oysters and fish west and brought fresh fruits and vegetables east.

A continuous parade of immigrants provided servants for the upper classes, encouraging ostentatious dinner parties of eight or ten courses. Appropriate wine accompanied each dish, which was based on a French recipe even when the cook was Irish.

Tea parties were in vogue and, during the summer, so were picnics. A popular entertainment for those near the ocean was a clambake. In a technique learned from Indians, fire was built in a stone-lined pit. When the fire died, the hot pit was filled with layers of seaweed, clams, crabs, lobsters and corn, then covered and used like an oven.

Rum Tum Tiddy

A version of Welsh rabbit (or rarebit) particularly favored in New England.

> 1 onion, chopped
> 1 tablespoon butter
> 2 ripe tomatoes, peeled, seeded and chopped
> 4 cups shredded Cheddar cheese
> 2 eggs, lightly beaten

Sauté the onion in the butter until golden. Add tomatoes to the onion and cook over medium heat until they bubble. Gradually stir in Cheddar cheese. When the cheese melts, stir in 2 lightly beaten eggs. Serve very hot over toast. Serves 2.

Finnan Haddie

A Scottish-English dish, finnan haddie came to America with the colonists. The name refers to the smoked haddock from Findhorn (Findon), a Scottish fishing port.

> 2 pounds smoked haddock
> 2 cups milk
> 1 cup water
> 1/2 cup heavy cream
> 2 tablespoons butter
> 1 tablespoon chopped parsley

Cut haddock into 4 pieces and place these in a heavy skillet. Add milk and water and bring slowly to a boil. Reduce heat and simmer for 12 minutes; turn over the haddock pieces and simmer 12 minutes longer. Transfer the haddock to a heated platter. Quickly measure the cooking liquid; return 1/2 cup to the skillet. Add cream, butter and chopped parsley. Stirring, boil this sauce for a minute. Pour over the haddock and serve, accompanied by boiled potatoes or hot toast. Serves 4.

The Mid-Atlantic States

In New York and Pennsylvania, early Dutch and German influence had made wursts, sauerkraut, crullers and doughnuts choice fare. Wheat and rye grew well, so these became the "bread colonies." Pennsylvania peaches were famous for quality and so plentiful they were fed to hogs, giving the pork superior flavor by some accounts.

In cities, food was lavish for the wealthy. New York City markets offered excellent pork and beef and more than sixty kinds of fish, many sold alive from tubs of seawater. The mile-long Philadelphia market was famed for fresh vegetables and fruits—and neatness. When the

United States acquired Florida from Spain in 1819, oranges and lemons went north. Pineapples were enjoyed by connoisseurs by 1830, but they were too expensive for most families.

Southern Cooking

The South was the home of America's first noted gourmet—Thomas Jefferson, who had traveled widely in France and Italy before becoming president and trying valiantly to refine American cookery. In Holland, he sampled waffles, and brought home a waffle iron. He introduced Neapolitan "maccaroni" (really, spaghetti) to America and served "French fries" with beef steak.

Jefferson brought an ice cream recipe back from France where the dessert is sometimes attributed to the chef of the Duc de Chartres. Although Dolley Madison gets credit for bringing ice cream to the White House, Jefferson introduced it there and, at one state dinner, served a precursor of baked Alaska: crisp hot pastry with ice cream inside.

Jefferson's elegant dining was not unique in the early United States. After Eli Whitney invented the gin, American exports of cotton leapt from half a million pounds in 1793 to ninety million in 1810 and reached almost two billion pounds in 1860. Enormous fortunes were made, enabling a lucky few to own huge plantations and grand town houses where they could live in luxury.

The South's biscuit soups, fried chicken, rice croquettes, puddings and endlessly varied desserts were much admired by visitors. Ward McAllister, a New York social leader, called the terrapin stew of Charleston and Savannah "a dish for the gods."

Along the coast, summer was celebrated with oyster roasts—a southern version of the

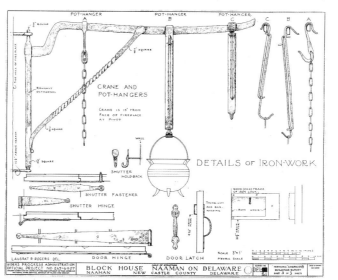

As shown in this schematic prepared in 1937 for the Historic American Buildings Survey, ironworks for the fireplace featured pot hangers of varying lengths, which allowed the housewife to position pots closer to the fire to boil food, or farther away from the heat to simmer. The blockhouse detailed in this drawing was built in 1654.

Spoon Bread

Every Southern family has the "best" recipe for spoon bread. Here's one of them:

2 cups milk	1/2 teaspoon salt
1 cup white cornmeal	4 eggs, separated
4 tablespoons butter	

Scald milk in the top of a double boiler over hot water. When bubbles form at the edges, gradually stir in cornmeal. Cook, stirring, until thick. Remove from the heat, stir in butter and salt. Beat egg yolks until frothy, add a little cornmeal to warm them, then stir the yolks into the cornmeal. Beat egg whites until stiff and fold them in. Pour into a buttered 6-cup baking dish and bake at 375°F for 40 minutes or until firm. Serves 4 to 6.

Sweet Potato Cake

1 cup butter or margarine, softened	3/4 teaspoon baking soda
2 cups sugar	1 teaspoon cinnamon
4 eggs	1/2 teaspoon nutmeg
2-3/4 cups cooked, mashed	1/2 teaspoon allspice
sweet potatoes	1/4 teaspoon salt
3 cups flour	2 teaspoons vanilla
2 teaspoons baking powder	1 cup chopped nuts (optional)

Cream butter and stir in sugar. Add eggs one at a time, beating well after each one. Add sweet potatoes and mix thoroughly. In a separate bowl, mix flour, baking powder, baking soda, cinnamon, nutmeg, allspice and salt. Slowly add flour mixture to sweet potato mixture, stirring well. Stir in vanilla. Add nuts, if desired. Pour batter into a greased, 10-inch tube pan. Bake for 1 hour, 10 minutes at 350°F or until done. Serves 10 to 12.

This 1854 lithograph entitled *Shake Hands?* by Lafosse (after an engraving by Mrs. L. M. Spenser) depicts the long hours a typical housewife spent preparing meals for her family, whether it be making a cake, tending the vegetable garden or defeathering a chicken.

clambake. Maryland cooks vied to produce the best crab cakes, while Carolina families treasured secret recipes for she-crab soup. In fine weather, families entertained by barbecuing whole steers or pigs—a practice some trace to the West Indian *barbacoa*, the name of a grid for roasting meat.

Creole Cooking

Steamboats that began plying the Mississippi about 1835 competed for the patronage of plantation owners, industrialists and gamblers by offering more elaborate fare than any city along the river. Their palatial, floating restaurants introduced northerners to southern and Creole-Cajun cuisine: tangy jambalaya and gumbo, chicory coffee and luscious pecan pralines—dishes reflecting both French and African influences.

Louisianans savored "crawdads," or crayfish, spiced their sausages with red peppers and served home-grown rice with red beans. Whether living in the delta or inland, they took advantage of the prodigality of the ocean and river that gave them pompano, redfish, shrimp, oysters, crabs, turtles and frogs.

Frontier Settlers in Minnesota—The Boelter Homestead, a wood engraving by F. O. C. Darley. As homesteaders cleared the land and plowed the prairies, the Midwest grew into the farm belt. The rich, loamy soil sprouted crops of wheat, corn, rye and barley, eventually becoming the nation's breadbasket.

The Heartland

When pioneers settled the Midwest, corn was usually the first crop planted because it provided food for both the farmer's family and his stock. Chickens in the farmyard supplied meat and eggs. In summer and autumn, fruits and vegetables came from a kitchen garden or were gathered wild to vary the menus.

The farmer's basic diet, however, was "hog and hominy," salt pork or bacon with cornbread or mush, supplemented by game or fish. The backwoods family relied on Providence for meat. Squirrel pie developed into a staple although hunters also might bring back

---

Charleston Benné Wafers

African slaves brought sesame (benné) seeds to South Carolina in the late 1600s. They are used in all manner of stews, cookies, candy and crackers.

1/2 cup benné seeds	1/2 teaspoon salt
2 cups flour	8 tablespoons butter
1 teaspoon baking powder	1/4 cup milk

Bake benné seeds at 325°F for about 5 minutes or until they are golden brown. Set them aside to cool. Combine flour, baking powder and salt. Rub in butter. Work in milk, then add the seeds. Chill the dough for at least 30 minutes, then roll it out 1/8-inch to 1/4-inch thick. Cut the dough into 2-inch disks and bake at 350°F for about 10 minutes or until the wafers are golden brown. Makes 4 to 5 dozen.

deer, bear, rabbit or porcupine. Special occasions in Kentucky called for "burgoo," a mixing of venison, rabbit and squirrel with beef, pork and mutton, plus whatever vegetables were found, all spiced with red pepper, cinnamon and cloves.

There were birds of every sort. In 1813 the American naturalist John James Audubon had witnessed a living "torrent" of passenger pigeons that lasted three days. But the pigeons were easily killed with net, trap, or blunderbuss—one farmer claimed he brought down 120 with one shot. They had disappeared from the East by 1850 and were becoming rare in the heartland. (A few captive birds lived until 1914.) Other species managed to survive although slaughtered by the thousands: turkey, plover, partridge and quail among them.

As farms prospered, plantings of wheat and rye followed corn, and cattle supplemented swine. By 1810, a livestock industry flourished in Ohio and Kentucky. Some animals were driven east; most were slaughtered and pickled or salted before shipping. Cincinnati, which was close to salt supplies and located on the Ohio River, became the leading packer. In the 1830s, it was named "Porkopolis" by local wags for having "perfected a system which packs 15 bushels of corn into a pig and packs that pig into a barrel and sends him over the mountains ... to feed mankind." Chicago, being closer to herds of cattle, was the major packer of grass-fed beef. Its first slaughterhouse opened in 1827.

With wheat and rye flour, cooks could bake breads and biscuits of different kinds. Fried beefsteaks appeared at breakfast as well as at dinner. Germans in cities like Milwaukee and St. Louis introduced hearty sausages, beer and dark bread.

In this 1913 drawing by Schmidt from *The Cabinet of American Illustration,* Washington Irving visits a Dutch housewife, perhaps looking forward to the results of her culinary talents. In his book *The Legend of Sleepy Hollow,* he described the delicacies to be found at a Dutch tea. "Such heaped-up platters of cakes of various and almost indescribable kinds, known only to experienced Dutch housewives! There was the doughty doughnut ... the crisp and crumbling cruller; sweet cakes and short cakes, gingercakes and honeycakes and the whole family of cakes."

While minister to France in the 1780s, Thomas Jefferson traveled widely in Europe and took an interest in food wherever he went. His notes on making "maccaroni" (spaghetti) show a drawing of a macaroni-making machine. The description ends by pointing out that the machine comes with a set of plates having "holes of different shapes desired for the different sorts of Maccaroni."

Corn Pone

This simple recipe went West with the pioneers.

2 cups cornmeal	4 tablespoons lard
dash of salt	3/4 cup boiling water
1/2 teaspoon baking soda	1/2–1 cup buttermilk

Sift together cornmeal, salt and baking soda into a bowl. Knead in lard. When well blended, add boiling water. Stir in enough buttermilk by the tablespoon to make a smooth dough. Form into 6 flat oval-shaped pones and arrange on a greased baking sheet. Bake at 350°F for 30 minutes or until firm and well browned. Serve hot.

WOLCOTT'S INSTANT PAIN ANNIHILATOR.

Fig 1. Demon of Catarrh. Fig 2. Demon of Neuralgia. Fig 3. Demon of Headache. Fig 4. Demon of Weak Nerves. Fig 5. 5 Demons of Toothache.

In 1863, Wolcott's Instant Pain Annihilator promised to cure headaches, weak nerves and toothaches, as well anything else that might bedevil a person. The alcohol content of patent medicines undoubtedly provided a sensation of well-being, though probably not to the degree that the manufacturers claimed for their miracle cures.

This whimsical lithograph entitled *Fish*— with the woman's skirt fashioned from a flounder, her hat a lobster, oyster shells for legs and other species of fish filling out the rest of the figure—depicts the variety of seafood available to cooks in the 1830s.

Communal chores—raising a barn, pulling out tree stumps, sewing quilts—were turned into "bees" with contests, races, dancing and desserts galore. In autumn when farm neighbors gathered to shuck corn or peel and slice apples for drying, a fiddle turned the occasion into a dance. In winter, skating and sleighing parties ended with dances and mugs of mulled cider. Sugaring-off called for a party, too. While grown-ups boiled the maple sap into syrup, children threw spoonfuls on the snow where it congealed into candylike "jack wax." Later came feasting and dancing.

The West

Starting in the 1840s, Mormons settled Utah, while other pioneers claimed farmlands in Oregon and Washington or tried to get rich quick in California's Gold Rush. After leaving Missouri's busy outfitting centers, settlers bound for Utah walked about 1,000 miles across treeless prairies and towering mountains. Those going to the West Coast marched almost twice as far.

Some areas boasted game: deer, antelope, elk, rabbits. Buffalo was prized, both fresh and "jerked" or turned into pemmican, an Indian invention of dried meat ground with berries and fat and wrapped in hide for long storage. Crossing rivers was a problem, but a supper of fish repaid the venturer. Wild plums, grapes and such were sometimes available; so was honey, for those who knew how to collect it.

After arriving in 1847, the Mormons soon irrigated the desert around the Great Salt Lake and developed a beneficence of fields and orchards. They produced food enough for themselves and for travelers who treated Utah as an oasis on their journey west.

Those who survived the ordeals of the Oregon trail found rich soil. Additionally, they discovered herds of deer, flocks of prairie chickens and schools of trout and salmon.

Meanwhile, gold turned California hamlets, especially San Francisco and Sacramento, into boom towns with all the luxuries money could buy, including fancy hotels, restaurants with French chefs and saloons selling imported liquors. But while a lucky few dined on breast of guinea hen, most Gold Rush prospectors settled for slumgullion, a watery stew of meat, potatoes and whatever vegetables could be rounded up.

The City Milk Business, an 1859 wood engraving published in *Harper's Weekly.* Domestic cows and goats provided milk to early settlers, but as towns and cities grew, fresh milk was delivered by milk wagons, the milkman ladling it out from large dairy cans. In 1885 the Borden Company began delivering milk door-to-door in bottles.

Canned Foods

The fundamentals of "canning" were formulated by France's Nicholas Appert in 1809. He "made the seasons stand still," according to a contemporary, by enclosing food in bottles, corking them tight and heating them in boiling water, which sterilized the food. In England, Peter Durand replaced breakable bottles with tin

Modern Domestic Cookery, written "by a Lady" and published in 1857, not only provided recipes but also illustrated the properly equipped kitchen.

cans (actually, steel lined with tin). By 1819, oysters, meat, vegetables and fruit were canned in America but were expensive and often poor in quality. They served chiefly as emergency travel rations.

In the 1840s, presses were patented to stamp cans from sheet metal, thus increasing a single worker's production tenfold.

Many middle-class housewives could then keep some canned goods at hand to add variety to menus. (It required ingenuity to get to the food until the first can opener was patented

---

Hangtown Fry

This omelet is said to have been invented during the Gold Rush at the Cary House restaurant in Hang Town, California—now called Placerville. The town got its original name from the public hangings held there.

1 dozen oysters	cracker crumbs
flour	butter
8 eggs	salt and pepper

For the fry, drain oysters, pat them dry and dredge them in flour. Beat 2 eggs, dip each oyster in the eggs, then roll it in cracker crumbs. Sauté the oysters in butter in a large skillet for 3 minutes or until brown on one side. Lightly beat 6 eggs; season with salt and pepper. Pour the eggs onto the oysters and cook for 2 minutes. Invert a heatproof plate over the skillet; carefully turn both over. Slide the omelet back into the skillet; cook until firm and golden brown. Serve with bacon. Serves 2 to 4.

This photo, taken in 1974 for the Historic American Buildings Survey, shows the kitchen at the late eighteenth century Mount Harmon Plantation near Earleville, Maryland. The kitchen was located in an outbuilding, a typical layout intended to keep the main house cool and odor-free.

in 1858 by Ezra J. Warner of Waterbury, Connecticut.) Families still depended on foods preserved at home, stocks that grew enormously after 1857 when John L. Mason invented an airtight top for his mason jar.

Side Dishes

Even more than the English, Americans were meat eaters. Many rarely touched vegetables, believing they caused disease, perhaps because they ripened in summer when epidemics were common. As a result, cooks who served vegetables often boiled them for hours.

The sweet potato flourished in southern gardens, but like the okra that Africans had brought with them, it was eaten mainly by slaves. White potatoes, discovered in Peru by the Spanish and brought by the English to the Carolinas in 1674, were not widely eaten until the nineteenth century—and then mostly in northern states.

Sweet corn was found in an Indian village on the banks of the Susquehanna in 1779. But the corn with soft sugary kernels proved a less predictable crop than hard flinty field corn, as it had since the days of the Incas. Not until the 1850s did selective breeding improve sweet corn enough to make it an important food crop in America.

At about the same time, American cooks began serving tomatoes. They were popular because they could be eaten raw as a salad (a new notion then) as well as stewed, broiled, scalloped or baked.

Cookstoves and Iceboxes

The first American patent for a cookstove went to the James Company in Troy, New York, in 1815. This prototype was only a cast-iron box with two stove lids on top. But refinements came fast, and by 1840, fireplaces were being boarded

---

Gloucester Chowder

Maine fishermen of the seventeenth and eighteenth centuries get credit for concocting this stew, named perhaps for a French cauldron called a chaudière.

4-pound cod or haddock	8 soda crackers
3 cups water	4 cups milk
1/4 cup diced salt pork	2–3 tablespoons butter
2 onions, sliced	salt and pepper
4 cups diced potatoes	

Have cod or haddock skinned. Remove the head, tail and backbone and simmer them in water for 20 minutes to make fish stock. Meanwhile, cut fish into 2-inch pieces and set aside. Fry salt pork until it renders its fat; add onions and cook until soft. Add pork and onions to stock and cook for 10 minutes. Strain into a deep pot, add the fish and potatoes; simmer for 15 minutes. Split soda crackers and soak them in 1 cup of the milk. When the potatoes are soft, pour remaining 3 cups milk into chowder, add butter and season with salt and pepper. Heat through. Place soaked crackers and their milk in a heated tureen. Pour in chowder. Serves 6 to 8.

up and replaced with iron stoves, especially in New England and the Mid-Atlantic states. After 1850, cookbooks assumed that anyone who could afford to buy a book would have a stove.

Cooking on the hearth, though, remained common in the South and in rural areas long after the Civil War. Some authorities believed cookstoves worsened American cuisine. Harriet Beecher Stowe wrote that "an open fireplace is an altar of patriotism. Would our Revolutionary fathers have gone barefooted and bleeding over snows to defend air-tight stoves and cooking-ranges?"

Not until the nineteenth century was ice-harvesting conducted on a large enough commercial scale so that ice and ice cream could be sold widely. Then huge insulated houses were built to hold the ice, which was cut into blocks of uniform size for easy handling. In 1803, a Maryland farmer named Thomas Moore patented the first domestic icebox. Most early models consisted of a wood cabinet with a tinned box inside holding shelves for food and, at the top, a metal-lined ice container. As ice melted, vents carried cool air down onto the food, and a tube led dripping water into a pan under the cabinet. By the 1830s, ice was accepted as an abundant, albeit expensive, household luxury.

"Dr. Chauncey's Patent Stove, 1846." The wood cookstove, first patented in 1815, gave home-makers much greater control over cooking, and it was safer, too, for they no longer had to work so close to skirt-singeing open fires.

Ice boxes kept food fresh and, more important, prevented perishables from spoiling. The first ice box, patented in 1803, was a wood cabinet lined with tin. A block of ice placed in a compartment at the top melted and cooled the interior. The drip pan underneath had to be emptied regularly, a chore often delegated to children. Ad from *Ballou's Pictorial Drawing-Room Companion,* 1855.

A Growing Formality

During the 1800s, a house of any size or pretension had a dining room separate from the kitchen. In

In rural areas, the farm wife still cooked in the fireplace. She started by selecting the right wood, usually oak or hickory, which burned evenly. Chestnut and hemlock had a tendency to explode, showering hot embers into the food or onto the cook. Block House, Naaman on Delaware, New Castle County, Delaware, built 1654. Photo taken for The Historic American Buildings Survey.

Cylindrical Mould.

Mould for Jellies of Mixed Colours.

whipped cream after the jelly is dished, which not only sets off the jelly, but is very good eaten with it. Also one for jellies of *mixed colours*, which is very pretty. These are filled with the jelly, coloured, and each layer allowed to get cold before the next is added. A little cochineal or sliced beet-root, with a few drops of lemon-juice, makes a beautiful red; spinach-juice, boiled with a small quantity of water to take off the rawness, makes a dark green.

CHAPTER XXV.

CONFECTIONERY.

693.—*Stove.*—In storerooms, or where there is not a char-coal stove for the purpose of preserving, the small portable French stove is found very convenient. A tin, with the sides a little turned up, should be placed under it; and there should be a free ventilation of air, as the best fuel for it is charcoal. It is lighted in the same way as a charcoal stove, by putting upon the bars a piece of charcoal already ignited; and may be put out by fixing the lid closely down. The French call it *un Fourneau Economique.* The original price is only a few shillings.

Stove for Preserving.

No longer simply a matter of survival, cooking was now considered an art, and much care went into the presentation of foods, as exemplified by these ornate molds illustrated in *Modern Domestic Cookery*, published by John Murray in 1857.

the homes of the wealthy, the table would seat at least twenty people—and did so regularly.

New emphasis on elegant dining at home created a market for tableware produced by American ceramic and pressed-glass makers, as well as for imports, mainly from English sources. Forks had become widely accepted by the end of the 1700s. The two-tined European style was soon replaced by a three-tined version, which in turn was quickly obsoleted by a fork with four tines. The table knife meanwhile was given a round end.

Formal dinners were grand affairs with a plethora of comestibles. Generally, the food was presented in two courses with twenty or more dishes laid out on the table at one time for each course. The first course would consist of savories—soups, meats, vegetables, bread—and the second of sweets such as fruits and cakes. At the end of the

Homemade bread required time and muscle. Some cook-books called for kneading the dough for forty-five minutes, while others required twice that, with the admonition that "any pause in the process injures the bread." While machine-made bread was quicker and cheaper (because fuel for cookstoves was expensive) most housewives still preferred to bake their own. This ad dates from 1858.

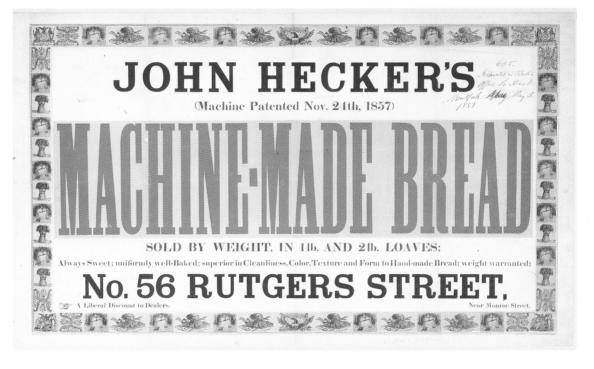

JOHN HECKER'S
(Machine Patented Nov. 24th, 1857)
MACHINE-MADE BREAD
SOLD BY WEIGHT, IN 1 lb. AND 2 lb. LOAVES:
Always Sweet; uniformly well-Baked; superior in Cleanliness, Color, Texture and Form to Hand-made Bread; weight warranted;
No. 56 RUTGERS STREET,
A Liberal Discount to Dealers.
Near Monroe Street.

meal, the ladies retired to the drawing room. The gentlemen adjourned to the host's study to drink port or brandy with their coffee and to smoke cigars.

American Cookbooks

When the first American cookbook appeared in 1796, its author, Amelia Simmons, styled herself "an American Orphan" although most of her recipes were borrowed from English books. She did include a handful of American innovations: cranberry sauce, pickled watermelon rind and five recipes using cornmeal—a johnnycake or hoecake, Indian slapjacks (pancakes) and three Indian puddings.

The Simmons book was reprinted and pirated for years, but within a few decades, new authors also made it clear that cooking had become Americanized—and regional. In 1824, Mary Randolph published *The Virginia Housewife*, introducing southern specialties such as catfish, beaten biscuits, gumbo and okra. During the 1830s, regional cookbooks included Mrs. Lettice Bryan's *The Kentucky Housewife* (1839); Philomelia Hardin's *Everybody's Cook and Receipt Book: But More Particularly Designed for Buckeyes, Hoosiers, Wolverines, Corncrackers, Suckers, and All Epicures Who Wish to Live with the Present Times* (Cleveland, 1842); Mrs. Esther Allen Howland's *The New England Economical Housekeeper* (Worcester, 1844) and *The Carolina Housewife*, By a Lady of Charleston (Charleston, 1847).

A trend of a different kind was set by the 1841 *Treatise on Domestic Economy* by Catherine Beecher, the first of the encyclopedic self-help manuals dealing with everything from rearing children to gardening. Her 1846 *Miss Beecher's Domestic Receipt Book* broke new ground by including instructions in cooking techniques along with recipes, thus providing a format for teaching "domestic arts" to later generations of schoolgirls.

Sauerkraut with Smoked Pork

2 pounds fresh sauerkraut	1 potato, finely chopped
1/2 cup chopped onion	1 tablespoon sugar
1/2 cup chopped tart apple	1/2 teaspoon ground allspice
1 tablespoon lard or drippings	pepper
2 cups cold water	2 pounds smoked pork or thick ham slice

Wash sauerkraut to remove excess salt; squeeze dry. In a heavy pot, sauté onions and apples in lard or drippings for 3 minutes, stirring often. When the onions are soft, stir in cold water, potato, sugar, allspice and a grating of pepper. Mix in the sauerkraut. Place smoked pork or ham slice on top of the sauerkraut. Cover, cook over low heat for 1-1/2 hours or until the meat is tender. Taste the sauerkraut, correct the seasoning and mound it on a hot platter. Slice the meat and arrange it around the sauerkraut. Serves 4 to 6.

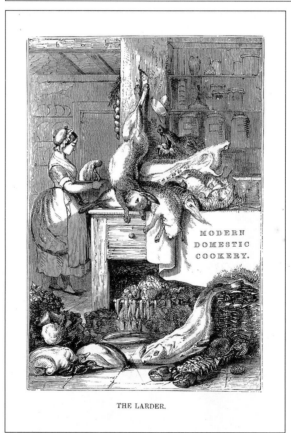

THE LARDER.

The frontispiece from *Modern Domestic Cookery*, published in the mid-1800s, shows the larder brimming with all manner of game, seafood and poultry.

After threshing, women shake the rice from the straw. Referred to as Carolina gold, rice was a major cash crop in southern coastal states, particularly North and South Carolina, where the rising and ebbing tides were used to flood and drain the rice fields. Illustration from *A Carolina Rice Plantation of The 1850s* by Alice R. H. Smith.

Snickerdoodles

1/2 cup butter, softened	1/2 teaspoon salt
3/4 cup sugar	1/2 cup milk
1 egg	1 teaspoon vanilla
2 cups flour	1/4 cup sugar
1-1/4 teaspoons baking powder	1 tablespoon cinnamon

Preheat oven to 325°F. Stir butter with a wooden spoon until creamy. Add sugar. Mix well. Add egg. Mix well. Mix flour, baking powder and salt in a separate bowl. Add one-third of the flour mixture to butter mixture. Stir well. Add half of the milk to the butter mixture. Stir well. Add half of the remaining flour mixture and rest of the milk. Stir well. Stir in the vanilla. Add the remaining flour mixture. Stir well. Drop heaping teaspoonfuls of dough about 2 inches apart onto a greased cookie sheet. Mix 1/4 cup sugar and 1 tablespoon cinnamon in a small bowl. Sprinkle sugar and cinnamon mixture over the mounds of dough. Bake 10 to 15 minutes or until cookies are lightly browned around the edges. Cool. Store in a tightly covered container. Makes 3 to 4 dozen cookies.

Temperance and Alcohol

Strong spirits were essential to every regional cuisine. By 1792, the United States supported some 2,597 distillers. Kentuckians turned corn into sour mash, sweet mash and bourbon (named for that county). Rum came from New England—where it remained the favored drink—and rye whiskey from the mid-Atlantic states.

The temperance movement started in New England in the early 1800s; by 1833 the American Temperance Union had eight thousand chapters. These pushed through state laws against the sale of alcoholic beverages, but most of the laws were declared unconstitutional—and all were unenforceable, as twentieth century Prohibitionists discovered in the 1920s. However, teetotalers widened the use of iced water and milk, although the purity of both was often questionable.

One temperance lecturer, Sylvester Graham, turned his attention to food in the 1830s. He espoused vegetarianism, claiming meats caused hot temper and sexual excess. He rejected white flour because it had been bolted (sifted) to remove its bran and germ. In boarding houses that he opened in New England, believers could enjoy meatless meals and whole-wheat bread. When he died in 1851, graham flour and graham crackers remained as his legacy.

This 1787 woodcut by Trenchard, published in *Columbia Magazine,* shows the rolling countryside of Delaware—well-tended farms with cows grazing in the pasture. At the time, nine out of ten people lived on farms.

Chapter Three
From Homemade to Store-Bought (1860–1900)

*D*uring the last decades of the nineteenth century, America was transformed from a rural to an industrial nation, stitched together by telegraph wires and transcontinental railroads. Products once fashioned by hand and at home—furniture, clothes, even foods—now were factory-made and store-bought.

More than 150 million acres of virgin soil were put under the plow, doubling America's cropland as native-born Americans, both black and white, joined immigrants from northern Europe—Ireland, Germany and Scandinavia mostly—to claim the Great Plains. During the 1880s and 1890s, immigrants came from southern and eastern Europe—Italy, Greece, Hungary, Poland, Russia. They sought work in factories, offices and stores, and crowded into cities in the prosperous North.

In 1860, America's population reached thirty million. By 1900, almost that many lived in cities alone. Total population soared to seventy-six million.

Entitled *A Fruit Market at Pittsburg,* this wood engraving by J. R. Brown shows a city marketplace, circa 1870, with melons and other produce piled high.

Store-Bought Food

Urban and rural families alike shopped for staples at general stores. There, tea and spices were scooped from tin boxes. Vinegar was drained from a keg with a spigot; crackers came in barrels and cheese in wheels. Even brand-name flour like Gold Medal was sold from 196-pound barrels.

Farmers grew most of the other foods they ate. City dwellers usually patronized specialized markets: butchers, poulterers, fishmongers, greengrocers, confectioners and bakers among them. Some communities boasted central marketplaces where venders supplied meat, fish, cheese and so on. In others peddlers hawked foods from pushcarts and horse-drawn wagons that traveled the streets and alleys.

Although the variety was limited, canned foods were popular. Canned goods let land-locked families enjoy shellfish and offered out-of-season fruits and vegetables. Travelers appreciated the convenience of already-cooked food. In 1860, canners sold about five million jars and cans of

Tomato catsup, previously homemade, could now be bought ready-made. Ad, published in 1900 by the U. S. Printing Company.

The bustling Washington Market in New York was crowded at Thanksgiving time, 1872. While general stores stocked staples, such as flour and sugar, women purchased fresh produce and meats directly from farmers who brought their goods to market in horse-drawn carts. Drawing by Jules Tavernier, published in *Harper's Weekly*, November 30, 1872.

This 1869 label for Pie Meat shows butchers preparing and chopping meats for canning. Canned meat and seafood allowed middle-class housewives to keep some on hand in the pantry, adding variety to the menu. The invention of the can opener followed soon after the advent of canning.

Along with ready-made foods came an increase in advertising, such as this 1899 ad for coffee.

food. With bulk orders from the Union Army during the Civil War, canners were able to build plants in the Midwest where the produce grew. Prices fell. Some thirty million units sold in 1870; by 1900, sales reached the billions.

The A&P

In 1859, George Gilman and George Huntington Hartford opened The Great American Tea Company in Manhattan to buy tea by the shipload and sell it directly to consumers. They believed they would make a profit by eliminating wholesalers and charging lower prices than other grocers charged. They were right.

Soon the firm offered coffee and spices and started to trade by mail. By 1869 Gilman and Hartford had the first grocery chain, with outlets in Boston and Philadelphia. That year they renamed the operation The Great Atlantic and Pacific Tea Company to commemorate the completion of the first transcontinental railroad. (Their own march west proved slow, not reaching the Pacific until 1930.) Gilman retired in 1878, but Hartford and his sons persevered. By 1900, A&P, as it was known, had almost two hundred stores, had put out its own brand of baking powder and had begun canning peas and tomatoes.

Dinner Parties, Teas and Drums

A wave of snobbery swept through the upper class during the last half of the nineteenth century when Americans were besotted by dreams of European aristocracy. Since France was touted as the font of culture in this "Age of Elegance," French food was necessary to exhibit one's social superiority.

A chef with a Gallic accent could make a fortune in New York or Boston; he also fared well in such places as Virginia City, Nevada, where prospectors struck it rich. Imported champagne and vintage Madeira were poured in the dining rooms of Chicago meat packers as well as those of Manhattan railroad magnates.

Dinner parties came into vogue. Invitations were engraved; individual menus were too, or written in calligraphy on porcelain. Tables were covered by lace and damask and set with crystal and fine china. Wealthy families bought gold service pieces; even modest households often accumulated an astonishing battery of silver that included tea sets and punch bowls.

Elaborate dinners consisting of seven courses and lasting two or three hours were presented in the latest mode: *service a la russe.* No longer did servants bring an array of soups, salads, roasts and side dishes to the table at one time in "the English style," leaving the host and hostess to carve and serve them. Now carving was done in the kitchen or at a sideboard by a butler, and the foods were passed by waiters—along with a different wine for each course.

Fewer serving dishes on the table meant hostesses had space for decorative centerpieces and individual bouquets or boutonnieres. Napkin folding turned squares of damask into swans, roses or lilies. (A continuous stream of immigrants willing to work as domestics enabled middle-class families to have one or two full-time servants. The rich might have four or five servants; twenty was not exceptional.)

Gradually, dinnertime shifted to late afternoon and then to early evening to accommodate the greater distances guests traveled within cities. Hungry ladies next popularized afternoon tea parties: low tea with simply a plate of thin sandwiches or cakes, or high tea featur-

A festive Christmas party, circa 1870, was made all the more festive by a Christmas punch spiked with alcoholic spirits.

Waldorf Salad

When the Fifth Avenue Waldorf Hotel opened in March 1893—at the site occupied since 1931 by the Empire State Building—the New York Symphony, led by the legendary conductor Walter Damrosch, provided music for the gala dinner. The menu was directed by maître d'hôtel Oscar Tschirky, who introduced 1500 of society's leaders from New York, Boston, Philadelphia and Baltimore to his latest creation: Waldorf Salad. His version contained two parts chopped tart apples to one part chopped celery, tossed with mayonnaise and served on lettuce leaves. Today, chopped walnuts—and, sometimes, chopped dates—enrich the mixture, while a dollop of lemon juice gives it an edge.

Asparagus in Ambush

For fancy luncheons, or as a first course at a dinner party, hostesses prided themselves on serving sauced vegetables encased in rolls. Asparagus and celery were favorites, but any firm vegetable would do, including carrots, celeriac, green beans, peas, even succotash of corn and lima beans.

     4 firm dinner rolls
     butter
     asparagus spears
     cream sauce or hollandaise sauce

Cut the tops from the dinner rolls and scoop out the crumbs from each one, leaving a case about 1/4-inch thick. Butter the cases and toast them, along with the tops, in a 350°F oven for about 5 minutes. Steam or simmer asparagus spears until barely tender. Cut the spears to fit inside the cases, then coat them with cream sauce or hollandaise sauce. Spoon the spears into the cases, set the tops over them, and bake the assembled rolls and asparagus for 2 or 3 minutes to heat them through. Serves 4.

Paid two dollars a week, Chinese laborers are shown in this 1879 wood engraving from *La Illistracion Española y Americana* pressing grapes in California. Spanish missionaries made wine from grapes they brought to California, where the dry summers were ideally suited for vineyards. In the 1850s wine production was a new industry; twenty years later some four million gallons flowed from vineyards in and around the Sonoma Valley.

ing more substantial foods such as creamed lobster in pastry. The ladies' tea was ancestor to the cocktail party, according to historian Russell Lynes. In the 1870s and 1880s, it was called a kettledrum; presumably the loud chatter resembled the rattle of that instrument.

Another favored entertainment was the evening musicale, which might center on a European string quartet in a Newport mansion or, in less privileged quarters, on a daughter of the house playing the spinet. At musicales, balls and other late parties, chicken and seafood salads bound with mayonnaise were customarily served. In *The American Salad Book* (1900), Maximilian De Loup decreed that chicken salad was "justly regarded as an American dainty."

Rural America was considerably less formal. Saturday was a time for church picnics, fish fries or barbecues in summer, covered-dish suppers in winter or pie sales where admirers shared their purchase with its baker.

Rhubarb Fool

Brought to America by early settlers who called it pie plant, rhubarb was specially prized because it appeared so early in spring. Field rhubarb is green-to-pink; modern hothouse types are pink-to-red. They taste alike.

1 pound rhubarb	1/4 cup water
1 cup sugar	1 cup heavy cream

Cut rhubarb into 2-inch pieces. (Discard leaves; these are poisonous.) Mix rhubarb with sugar and water in glass or stainless steel pot; simmer for 30 minutes until very tender. Drain rhubarb in a colander; press rhubarb through food mill or puree in processor. Chill well. Whip cream until stiff, stir in rhubarb and serve cold in stemmed glasses. Serves 4 to 6.

Key Lime Pie

When condensed milk became widely available after the Civil War, this easy version of Key Lime Pie appeared. Although some bakers consider true Key limes indispensable, others substitute plain limes—or use lemons.

2 eggs, separated
1/2 teaspoon cream of tartar
1/4 cup sugar
1 15-ounce can sweetened condensed milk
1/2 cup Key lime juice
1 tablespoon grated lime peel

Beat egg whites with cream of tartar until almost stiff, slowly add sugar and continue beating until the whites are stiff. Set this meringue aside. Mix the sweetened condensed milk with grated lime peel and lime juice. Add egg yolks and stir until the mixture thickens. Pour into a baked 9-inch pie shell. Spread meringue on top and bake at 350°F for 10 minutes or until the pie is golden brown.

Safe Milk

During the 1880s and 1890s, vendors sold milk door-to-door in cities, scooping it out of huge dairy cans. Often they sold watery "swill milk" from cows fed cheaply on brewers' wastes; chalk masked its yellow color.

In the 1860s, French scientist Louis Pasteur demonstrated that heat killed microbes in milk. However, many physicians argued that instead of being pasteurized, milk should be certified as coming from clean dairies with disease-free cows. Three decades later, scientists were still debating.

One advocate of pasteurizing was New York philanthropist and Macy's owner, Nathan Straus. Ignoring the debates, he took action and subsidized summer milk stations in Manhattan tenements in 1892, giving away bottled, pasteurized milk and teaching mothers to boil milk at home. As he hoped, death rates among infants and children fell dramatically. Straus carried his message across America and to Europe. Cincinnati led the way in requiring pasteurization in 1897.

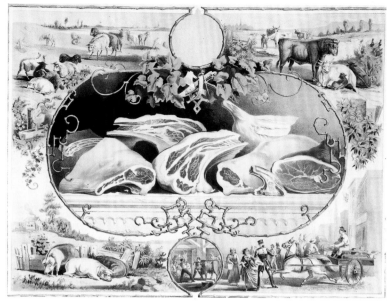

The Best in The Market, an 1872 lithograph by H. Thomas, published by Kimmel and Voight, shows the before and after of various kinds of meat—both on the hoof and dressed and cut for sale. Americans, like the English, were a nation of meat-eaters.

After a harrowing Atlantic crossing where he saw babies sicken and die for lack of pure milk, Connecticut dairyman Gail Borden set about finding a way to preserve milk by adding sugar and heating it in a vacuum. Borden got his first patent in 1853, and less than a decade later, his plants were supplying the Union Army with floods of canned condensed milk, thus introducing the product to a wide market.

In 1880, Swiss Johann Baptiste Meyenberg discovered how to can unsweetened milk. After immigrating to America in 1885, he set up the Helvetia Milk Condensing Company—later called the Carnation Company—in Highland, Illinois.

Wondrous White Bread

No matter how often millers sifted, flour always held flecks of brown until the 1870s when steam-powered equipment was developed to crush wheat and winnow out all middlings—bran and germ. About the time whiteness became a possibility, Russian Mennonites brought to Kansas seeds of a hard spring wheat with the high gluten content needed for good bread flour.

While flour improved, so did leavening. Traditionally, bakers had relied on brewers' or sourdough yeast, both variable in quality. In the 1800s, they experimented with pearlash (a mild lye made from wood

Recipes for beers and ales came to America with the early colonists. The first public brewery was opened by the Dutch in New Amsterdam. When German immigrants arrived, beer gardens became popular. *The Connoisseur,* a chromolithograph, dates from the 1880s.

2. GATEAU.
3. RIBBON JELLY.
4. DOMINOES.

5. NEAPOLITAN PASTRY.
6. VANILLA CREAMS.
7. CHEESE CANAPEES.

1. RUSSIAN CHARLOTTE.

ash) and salteratus (a form of baking soda), but these alkalis were unreliable and made food taste soapy unless they were neutralized with an acid like buttermilk.

Reliable baking powders, combining soda and cream of tartar or tartaric acid, did not appear until the 1850s and 1860s. Then in 1867, Charles and Maximillian Fleischmann immigrated from Austria to Cincinnati with an effective, predictable yeast that the brothers soon were reproducing for sale in compressed cakes.

Bakeries thrived. By the turn of the century, about a quarter of all bread was store-bought. The new smooth white bread yielded uniform slices that encouraged sandwich-making. Cooks tried all kinds of fillings: egg salad, sardines, watercress, jam and lobster salad, to name a few. Texans invented the open toasted cheese sandwich. With uncanny timing, Underwood's Red Devil Ham Spread appeared in 1868. The club sandwich featuring three slices of toast, chicken, bacon, tomato and lettuce was devised, according to historian John Mariani, about the turn of the century and dubbed clubhouse sandwich for the men's social clubs that popularized it.

Cattlemen and Meat Packers

During the 1860s, hundreds of thousands of longhorns, descended from cows that the Spanish brought to America, roamed Texas. Cattlemen found that the Great Plains were pastures where cows could feed themselves and, according to one Texan, "make the dollars crawl into your jeans."

Actually, longhorns sold for as little as one dollar a head until railroads with connections to Chicago and points east reached Kansas in 1867, and cattlemen could drive herds north along the six-hundred-mile Chisholm Trail to sell in Abilene or Dodge City. The trip required two months or more, but some ten million animals made it before the Missouri, Kansas & Texas Railroad crossed the Red River in 1885. After that, cattle took a short trip to a Texas railhead.

At first, railroads took live cattle east for slaughter. In 1869, George H. Hammond of Detroit had a refrigerated car built for dressed beef. Packers Gustavus F. Swift, Philip D. Armour and Michael Cudahy followed suit from Chicago, which already was a railroad hub. By the 1880s, refrigerator cars were carrying dressed beef nationwide.

Longhorn beef was as tough as its travels. But it sold. Within a few decades, though, the lanky grass-fed longhorns were replaced by Herefords and Black Angus, fattened (or finished) on corn in Midwest feed lots to yield tender steaks and roasts.

After depending on the pig for sustenance for generations, Americans now generally rejected it except in ham. Upper-class diners not only ranked fresh pork below beef, but also below

Even with early ice boxes, it was not uncommon to snack standing in front of the open door as the young man in this 1897 photo, *After the Ride,* is doing.

Bishop Whipple's Dessert

An Episcopalian bishop of the mid-1800s, Henry Whipple lent his name to several sweets. Born in New York, he served as a bishop in Minnesota.

2 eggs	1 cup chopped dates
1/3 cup sugar	1 cup chopped pecans
2/3 cup flour	1–2 tablespoons sweet sherry
1 teaspoon cinnamon	1 cup heavy cream
1/2 teaspoon nutmeg	2 tablespoons superfine sugar
1 teaspoon baking powder	

Beat eggs with sugar, flour, cinnamon, nutmeg and baking powder. When smooth, stir in chopped dates and pecans. Spread the batter in a buttered baking dish and bake at 350°F for 20 to 30 minutes or until firm and golden. Cool. Break into small pieces and sprinkle evenly with sweet sherry. Beat heavy cream until almost stiff; beat in superfine sugar. Top dessert with whipped cream. Serves 4 to 6.

A popular snack food by 1855, popcorn was one of the varieties of corn originally cultivated by Native Americans. Legend has it that at the end of the Thanksgiving meal, they surprised the colonists with this native treat. This Denver, Colorado, street scene was photographed in 1895.

Spotted Dog

Even a campfire cook could produce this simple dessert.

> 1/2 cup rice
> 1/2 cup brown sugar or molasses
> 1/2 cup raisins
> 4 cups milk

Combine rice and brown sugar or molasses with milk. Stir in raisins. Simmer slowly for 30 or 40 minutes until the rice is tender and has absorbed most of the milk. Serves 4 to 6.

mutton and poultry. Innards such as tongue, kidneys, brains and sweetbreads were reckoned choice morsels. Veal and lamb, on the other hand, never found broad acceptance. City dwellers found those meats relatively expensive because farmers were reluctant to slaughter "baby" animals—partly because of sentiment, partly because mature stock was heavier and brought in more money.

Hunters pose with their take of game birds in the Dakotas at the end of the nineteenth century. When settlers first arrived on American shores, the skies were reportedly darkened by flocks of birds. Overhunting, however, drastically reduced a number of species; the passenger pigeon was extinct by the turn of the century.

Bird in the Hand

Chickens were so easy to raise that most families kept some if they had a bit of land. Like the pig, the chicken fed itself and was fairly docile. Not so the temperamental turkey, which needed feed and fence. It was a Thanksgiving treat accompanied by cranberry sauce. At Christmas, families might enjoy a second turkey or a goose—another holiday-only kind of bird.

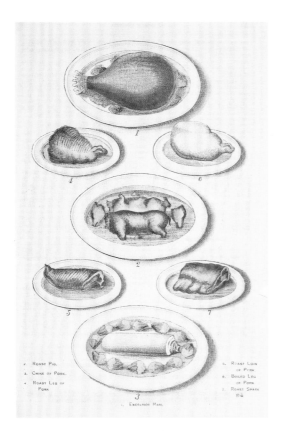

Left—*The Household Treasure,* an 1871 cookbook, shows various cuts of pork, the main source of meat for Americans because "the hog costs nothing to keep." The movement of settlers to the Midwest and the South was sustained largely on a diet of "hogs and hominy."

Right—In *Hot Roasted Chestnuts,* an 1891 drawing by Arthur Burdett Frost, roasted chestnuts are poured directly into a gentleman's pocket for snacking on the go.

Left—Traditional English fare, such as mincemeat and plum pudding touted in this 1876 ad, remained popular even as Americans' tastes expanded.

Right—Fruit extracts were used for flavoring desserts, ice creams and jellies.

Chicken à la King

What King? Perhaps E. Clarke King II, who owned the Brighton Beach Hotel in Brighton Beach, Long Island, during the end of the nineteenth century. The creator is said to be Chef George Greenwald. Here is a modern version:

6 tablespoons butter	1 cup green pepper strips
3 tablespoons flour	3 cups diced cooked chicken
2 cups chicken broth	1/2 cup chopped pimiento
2 cups light cream	2 egg yolks, beaten
1 cup sliced mushrooms	1/2 cup dry sherry

Melt 4 tablespoons of the butter in a saucepan. Stir in flour, then chicken broth and light cream. When the sauce thickens, set it aside to cool slightly. Sauté mushrooms and pepper strips in remaining 2 tablespoons butter until softened. Add chicken and pimiento. Stir a little cooled sauce into 2 beaten egg yolks, then stir egg yolks into remaining sauce. Add to chicken mixture and cook over low heat until heated through. Off the heat, stir in sherry. Serve over rice or hot toast or in pastry shells. Serves 6.

Ducks were eaten more frequently. In 1873, a clipper ship captain brought back white Peking ducks as a gift for a friend on Long Island, New York. The birds flourished to spawn an industry in what became Long Island ducklings.

The ring-necked pheasant, which gourmets have long considered the best-flavored game bird, is Asian. Thomas Jefferson and Richard Bache (Benjamin Franklin's son-in-law) tried, unsuccessfully, to raise them. In 1881, Owen N. Denny, former American consul in Shanghai, released fifty or sixty pheasants on his Oregon farm. The birds did so well there that during the first hunting season, ten years later, some fifty thousand were bagged on opening day.

Diminishing Shellfish

New England's famed lobsters had become delicacies by the 1890s; its oysters were small, but still prized. Hardshell clams were abundant, as were softshells. Only Italian or Portuguese immigrants collected the ubiquitous mussel.

Maryland's diamond-back terrapin was nearly gone from the Chesapeake Bay. However, its clams and blue crabs seemed inexhaustible, as did oysters and crabs farther south and along the Gulf of Mexico. On the Pacific coast were tiny Olympia oysters, hefty Dungeness crabs and abalone. In the 1880s, entrepreneurs had little success when they tried to transplant eastern oysters to San Francisco waters, but Atlantic softshell clams inadvertently harvested with the oysters thrived in the Pacific.

Blackberry Grunt

Berries of any kind can be used for this recipe, making it a favorite of pioneer families who relied on wild fruit for desserts.

1 cup flour	2 cups berries
2 teaspoons baking powder	1/2 cup sugar
1/2 teaspoon salt	1 cup water
1/2 cup light cream or buttermilk	

Sift together flour, baking powder and salt. Pour in cream or buttermilk and stir until the batter is smooth. In a heavy glass, enameled or stainless steel saucepan, mix berries with sugar and water. Bring the berries to a boil over high heat. Cook for a minute or so, then drop the batter by the tablespoonful into the berries, spacing these dumplings about an inch apart. Cover tightly and simmer undisturbed for 20 minutes or until the dumplings puff and a toothpick inserted into one comes out clean. Transfer the dumplings to 6 bowls and spoon berries over and around them. Serves 6.

America's Sweet Tooth

Many Americans saw, and ate, their first banana at the 1876 Philadelphia Centennial Exposition where the fruit was sold—wrapped in tinfoil—at a dime apiece. Imported from Jamaica, bananas had rarely traveled inland from the eastern seaboard.

As the railroad network grew, fruit was among the first foods shipped. Refrigerated cars turned the Carolinas and gulf states into strawberry growers; Colorado produced cantaloupe; peaches came from Georgia. California oranges, chiefly seedless navels, went east by carloads after 1876.

Whatever else was on the table, Americans wanted a dessert. In rural areas, pies commonly were served both noon and night. So great was their appeal that frontier wives created an "apple pie made with soda crackers" in which broken crackers flavored with lemon replaced apple slices.

During the 1880s and 1890s, rich plum pudding and mincemeat pie gave way to lighter tapioca or custard. Jellied desserts became the rage after Charles B. Knox introduced packaged powdered gelatin in 1893. Soon Pearl B. Wait and Orator Woodward brought out Jell-O for fruity, shimmering molds.

Before the Civil War, bakers turned out pound cakes, spicy fruit cakes and gingerbread—confections that were close to fail-safe in a fireplace oven. Using the superior oven of an iron stove, with finer flour and leavening, bakers expanded their repertories. First came layer cakes, then jelly rolls and finally angel food. Strawberry shortcake with a biscuit base found favor in the 1880s, probably because baking powder finally was available to help housewives produce fluffy biscuits.

After the Civil War, ice cream was molded and flavored and colored many ways by confectioners and ice cream parlors. Robert M. Green introduced ice cream sodas at the 1874 Semicentennial Exhibition in the Franklin Institute in Philadelphia. And in the 1890s, Ed Berner of Two Rivers, Wisconsin, is said to have created the sundae on that day of the week.

At home, cooks cranked out ice cream with the aid of the portable churn that American Nancy Johnson, wife of a naval officer, had invented in 1846. All they needed, besides endurance, were chipped ice and rock salt. The simplest recipe called for thick cream, sugar and a flavoring such as crushed fruit or vanilla. When egg custard replaced or supplemented the cream, Neapolitan ice cream was the reward.

Fudge was invented in the last decades of the century to the delight of college girls, among others. Vassar fudge was cooked up from chocolate, cream, sugar and butter. At Smith College, students sweetened it with brown sugar and molasses; Wellesley added marshmallows. Rebecca

Orange Ambrosia

6 large navel oranges
confectioners' sugar
2 cups grated coconut

Peel and segment 6 large navel oranges; remove the membranes. Place half of the oranges in a serving bowl, sprinkle lightly with confectioners' sugar and about 1 cup grated coconut. Add the remaining oranges, some sugar and another cup of coconut. Cover and refrigerate for at least 4 hours to chill well. In parts of the South, ambrosia is a traditional Christmas dessert. Serves 4 to 6.

This 1872 Currier and Ives lithograph depicts sugaring time in New England, when families worked together to tap the trees and gather the sap. The boiling off process continued for days, reducing thirty-five gallons of sap to one gallon of syrup.

Sophia Clarke's *Dotty Dimple Stories* featured taffy made from sugar and vinegar; like the books, taffy became an American favorite, and taffy pulls developed as a popular entertainment for teenagers.

New Ideas about Breakfast

Traditional farm breakfasts were as hearty—and meaty—as dinners. Citified Americans ate more sparingly, so bacon and eggs or porridge and fruit replaced steaks.

Quaker Oats was created during the 1890s by millers who calculated that packaged cereal would outsell the bulk kind. They used the name Quaker to signal wholesomeness. The invention of Cream of Wheat was serendipitous. Emery Mapes, a miller in Grand Forks, North Dakota, attempted to produce a new kind of wheat flour. What he invented was lumpy as flour, but proved to be a best-seller when advertised as a hot cereal in 1895.

The first cold cereal probably was invented by Dr. John H. Kellogg, a Seventh-Day Adventist vegetarian, who became manager of the group's Battle Creek, Michigan, sanitarium (called the San) in 1876. Working with his brother Will K. Kellogg, he created a food that he called "granula"—stale bread, dried in the oven, then ground up. Later they produced flaky wheat and corn cereals by baking bits of boiled paste in the oven. Will finally bought the commercial rights to the corn flakes, perked them up by adding sugar, salt and malt, then wrapped them in waxed paper to keep them fresh.

At about the same time, Shredded Wheat was introduced by Denver lawyer Henry Perky, looking to get rich by baking strands of boiled wheat, shaped like baskets. (He did get rich. He also invented Triscuit crackers.) Charles W. Post cured his own ulcers with Grape-Nuts he developed by baking wheat and barley bread, shredding the loaves, then baking the shreds and grinding them into "nuts." (Why called grape? Nobody knows. The cereal's original name had been "Elijah's manna"—heretical, some thought.)

Fried Apples and Onions

1 pound thick sliced bacon
6 onions, thinly sliced
6 tart apples

Fry bacon slices until crisp. Drain on absorbent paper. Pour off all but a few spoonfuls of fat from the skillet and add onions. After 2 or 3 minutes, add apple rings made from apples, cored and sliced thick but not peeled. Stir gently, reduce the heat, cover and cook for 5 to 10 minutes until the apples are tender. Serve with the bacon.

Kitchen Convenience

Cast-iron stoves fueled with wood or coal dominated Victorian kitchens, enabling cooks to regulate heat with fair precision. Gas stoves were exhibited by the 1850s, but because of the potential danger were rare even in the 1890s. The electric stove at the 1893 Columbian Exposition in Chicago was a marvel of science, not a usable appliance.

Small gadgets proliferated: a hand-operated meat grinder, a rotary eggbeater, an apple corer and cherry pitter, a juice extractor. The grinder proved especially important because it quickly minced meat, seafood and vegetables for hash and the croquettes then in style.

Chafing dishes came into vogue during the 1890s. Formerly made of inexpensive metal, they now appeared in copper and silver as grand additions to a buffet table. Sauced dishes like chicken à la king could be kept warm for hours. And by doing a little advance work in the kitchen, a hostess

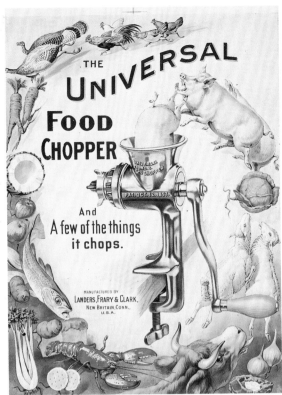

Left—Entitled *Overindulgence—A Spoiled Thanksgiving,* this illustration by Stephens appeared in *Harper's Weekly* in 1896. An ingrained Puritan ethic considered it sinful to eat to excess.

Right—Precursor to the Cuisinart, the Universal Food Chopper could grind many kinds of foods. It was one of numerous kitchen gadgets invented during the late 1800s, gadgets such as eggbeaters, apple corers and cherry pitters.

In addition to ice boxes, cookstoves and store-bought foods, the Industrial Revolution brought in the home washing machine, as shown in this 1869 lithograph, making the housewife's life easier.

An 1897 advertisement for Red Messina Orange employs a touch of humor to illustrate several uses for the flavoring.

Bitter herbs were used to mask the taste of alcohol in various brands of rejuvenating tonics, like the one recommended in this 1859 ad. Using alcohol for medicinal purposes goes back to early colonists, whose folk remedies nearly always included spirits. A cold, for instance, could be treated with cherries soaked in rum, or with ginger tea mixed with honey and whiskey.

with dramatic flair could turn cooking rarebit or scrambled eggs into what Fannie Farmer called a "merry feast."

Cookbooks and Cooking Schools

During the Civil War, church and charity societies invented a unique American kind of cookbook—the fund-raiser—sold then at so-called Sanitary Fairs to raise money for military hospitals and medical supplies. After the war, these "charitable cookbooks" were compiled to benefit libraries, churches, orphanages and the like.

The original Sanitary Fair cookbooks were simple paperbound affairs, often only ten or twelve pages long. The recipes were contributed by local women and some were closely guarded family secrets. Over the years, charity books grew in numbers of pages and copies. Many lifted recipes from other books. They often included ads to raise extra money. Cookbook authority Jan Longone estimates that more than three thousand such books appeared between the Civil War and World War I.

In the late 1860s, interest in cooking was piqued when women's magazines such as *Godey's Lady's Book* began to publish articles about food. New magazines such as *Household* (1868–1903), *Woman's Home Companion* (1873–1957), *Ladies' Home Journal* (1883) and *Good Housekeeping* (1885) ran menus and recipes, teaching new cooks and giving everybody new pride in their culinary achievements.

High schools began to teach domestic arts. And private cooking schools appeared to help both housewives and their servants. In 1874, Juliet Corson opened the New York Cooking School. Sarah E. Hooper started its Boston counterpart in 1879; Mary Johnson Lincoln was the first principal, followed by Fannie Merritt Farmer, who set up her own school in 1902. Maria Parloa taught in Boston, but is remembered as food editor of *Good Housekeeping*, a post she held for many years.

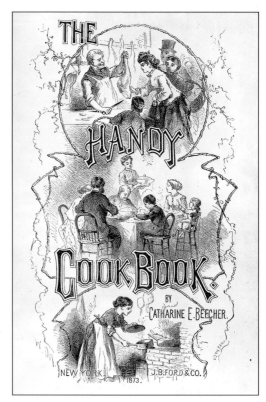

The Handy Cook Book by Catherine E. Beecher was one of numerous volumes and treatises she wrote for homemakers. She advocated educating women in household management and collaborated with her sister, Harriet Beecher Stowe, on a book entitled *The American Woman's Home; or, Principles of Domestic Science* (1869).

The *Ladies' Home Journal* first appeared in 1883. This women's periodical printed recipes and advice for the "practical housekeeper."

Cape Cod Turkey

Long after wild turkeys had disappeared from the Cape, there were fish to bake for dinner.

> 4 pound cod
> butter
> 1 onion, chopped
> 1-1/2 cups coarse bread crumbs
> 1/2 cup chopped celery
> 2 tablespoons chopped parsley
> 1/2 cup milk, water or fish stock

Have the cod cleaned and—if the fishmonger is skilled—get the backbone removed, but leave the head and tail intact. Wash the cod inside and out. Wipe it dry and rub in oil or melted butter. Sauté onions in 2 tablespoons butter until pale golden. Stir in bread crumbs, celery and parsley. Moisten with milk, water or fish stock. Lightly press this stuffing into the cod; sew up its cavity and place it on an oiled rack in a large baking pan. Bake at 450°F for 10 minutes per inch of thickness, measured at the thickest part. Transfer cod to a serving platter and garnish with parsley. Serves 6.

In books and magazine articles, these teachers spread their knowledge of cooking, nutrition, kitchen arrangement, and table setting. Most cookbooks described vegetarian foods and care for invalids. In almost all, desserts filled more than half the pages.

The best seller proved to be Fannie Farmer's *The Boston Cooking-School Cook Book* that debuted in 1896. Farmer's prose was terse and direct. And she measured ingredients precisely. Measuring spoons and cups had been introduced in the 1880s, but it was Fannie Farmer who authoritatively dismissed the "heaping teaspoon" or "scant cupful" that had been so confusing for generations of novices. She called for leveling spoons and cups with a knife, and is still remembered as the "Mother of Level Measurements."

A Friday Night in the Jewish Quarter, an 1889 illustration by W. A. Rogers published in *Harper's Weekly*, shows an immigrant selling apples from a cart. The influence of other cultures increased dramatically during the late 1800s, when waves of immigrants arrived from Italy, Greece, Hungary, Poland and Russia.

Soda Fountain Drinks

During the late 1700s, some clever Swiss had found out how to "aerate" ordinary water by bubbling carbon dioxide through it. The English dubbed the drink "soda water"—perhaps because it fizzed like water mixed with sodium bicarbonate (baking soda)—and soon sweetened and flavored it, first with lemon and then with ginger. In the 1830s, John Matthews introduced soda water to Americans. Soda stands or "street spas" quickly started selling the bubbly water, plain or mixed with flavored syrups.

Pharmacies began selling soda, calling it a tonic to cure dyspepsia. After the Civil War, they installed marble-topped counters from which to dispense soda water, perhaps spiked with phosphoric acid to create a tingly phosphate.

Philadelphia pharmacist Charles E. Hires marketed a sweet, carbonated herb tea in 1876. He called it "rootbeer," hoping men would buy it. Aggressive advertising expanded sales with claims like "Hires Rootbeer gives the children strength to resist the enervating effects of the heat." (The Women's Christian Temperance Union, however, boycotted his beer until a lab test showed that it was no more alcoholic than bread.)

In 1886, Atlanta pharmacist Dr. John Styth Pemberton created the syrup for that most famous of soda fountain drinks: Coca-Cola, combining extracts of the African kola nut with those of coca. (After 1903, Coca-Cola used drug-free coca.) In 1891, Asa Candler bought the formula and began advertising the drink. Bottling started three years later, but large-scale production was not possible until the turn of the century when crimped-on bottle caps were invented. Meanwhile, in 1896, Caleb D. Bradham of New Bern, North Carolina, had added Pepsi-Cola to the soda fountain lineup.

War Gardens, drawing by Alice Barber Stephens, circa 1917. As the United States entered World War I, many foods became scarce and rationing was imposed. To help the war effort, civilians were encouraged to plant "liberty gardens" in their backyards.

Chapter Four
The Age of Optimism (1900–1920)

*T*he twentieth century began with peace and general prosperity. Science was the key to progress, which would raise the standard of living for everyone. America was the world's leading industrial power. Railroads sped across it and, after 1915, so did telephone calls.

The farmer and businessman were doing well. Taxes were low; trade was brisk. Stores were well-stocked and food, affordable: eggs cost a penny apiece and sirloin steak only 24 cents a pound.

Typewriters and telephones expanded women's job opportunities. Wives as well as spinsters took positions as stenographers, clerks and telephone operators. In 1920 some 8.5 million women were gainfully employed; that year women won the right to vote.

The Four-Course Dinner

Gracious living was paramount for middle-class American women although domestic servants were growing hard to find as immigrant women discovered better-paying jobs elsewhere. Most house-wives did all or most of the work of creating meals for their families and friends.

Entertaining at home at luncheons and dinners was fashionable nonetheless. Women met for formal teas, gave theme parties and joined dinner clubs to show off cooking skills. When guests came, housewives assembled four-course dinners like those described in magazines and popular cookbooks: soup, meat or fish with potatoes and vegetables, salad and dessert.

Although beef probably was what husbands craved, middle-class wives acquired a white-food mania not satisfied by white bread, white rice and white sugar. In a perfect meal, everything must be the color of snow, smothered by sauce and bland to the point of flavorlessness. One suggested menu consisted of celery soup, poached chicken breast, mashed potatoes, cauliflower, jellied-fruit-and-ginger-ale

Crab Louis

Around the turn of the century, a San Francisco chef—whether at the St. Francis Hotel or at Solari's restaurant is not certain—devised this presentation for the Pacific's magnificent Dungeness crab.

> 1 pound cooked or defrosted crabmeat
> 2 ripe avocados
> 1 cup mayonnaise
> 1/2 cup heavy cream
> 1/4 cup chili sauce
> 1/4 cup chopped scallions
> 2 tablespoons chopped green olives
> 2 teaspoons fresh lemon juice
> red pepper

Drain and pick over crabmeat; tear it into bite-sized pieces. Halve, peel and pit avocados. Combine mayonnaise, heavy cream, chili sauce, chopped scallions, green olives, lemon juice and a few grains of red pepper. Stir in the crabmeat. Spoon the crab mixture into the avocado halves and present on lettuce leaves. Serves 4.

salad with mayonnaise and rice pudding with vanilla sauce.

Farmers introduced iceberg lettuce, developed to withstand handling and shipping, in 1903. It was close to colorless and tasteless—ideal for salad.

In most kitchens spices were little used except for parsley, which seemed ubiquitous; herbs were rare. Food writers preached decorative presentation, thus complicating cookery for amateurs. The highest praise these Edwardians could bestow was to call a dish "dainty." Even the otherwise sensible Fannie Farmer doted on such fripperies as cock's-comb-shaped croutons and radishes cut to resemble fuschias.

Molded salads were stylish. One popular type, according to food historian Laura Shapiro, was the perfection salad that won third prize in a 1905 contest sponsored by Knox Gelatin: chopped celery, cabbage and sweet red peppers bound by plain aspic—or, in later versions, tomato aspic.

Provisions

Ambitious cookery was simplified by the grocer's stock of affordable canned and packaged goods. Campbell's condensed tomato soup went on the market at the turn of the century; other soups followed. Spinach and peas were canned by 1900; olives, by 1901; pineapple, by 1910; mushrooms, by 1918. Tuna canneries started in 1903.

Refrigerated railroad cars whisked fresh fruits, vegetables, meats and fish across the country—

In 1908 General Electric brought out the electric toaster; the next year they promoted a toaster-stove for "breakfast without going into the kitchen."

Vichyssoise

When the old Ritz-Carlton Hotel in Manhattan opened a Roof Garden Restaurant in 1917, Chef Louis Diat concocted this cold version of a hot leek-and-potato soup he remembered from his childhood. At the Ritz the menu listed the soup as Crême Vichyssoise Glacée.

4 leeks	2 cups milk
1 onion, chopped	2 cups light cream
2 tablespoons butter	1 cup heavy cream
4 cups chicken stock	chives
5 medium potatoes, sliced thin	

Combine the chopped white parts of leeks with onion and cook in butter in a large pot until soft. Add boiling chicken stock and potatoes. Simmer for 30 to 40 minutes. Puree through a food mill or sieve. Return the puree to the pot. Stir in milk and light cream. Season to taste. Bring to a simmer. Refrigerate until cold. To serve, stir in heavy cream. Garnish each serving with finely cut fresh chives. Serves 8.

Her Face was Dark with Sweat and Streaked with Perspiration, appeared in the August 1912 issue of the *Ladies' Home Journal*. Still published today, the *Journal* was one of numerous women's magazines that came out in the late 1800s, along with magazines such as *Woman's Home Companion* and *Good Housekeeping*.

Sides of meat hang in a Chicago butcher shop in 1901. Convenient to the farms and ranches of the Midwest, Chicago became the country's meat packing capital with refrigerated railway cars transporting meat across the nation.

at a price. In the Midwest, the wealthy might indulge in avocados (called alligator pears) or live lobsters. By 1903, refrigerator ships brought bananas to Atlantic and Gulf ports whence they went north and west by rail. California artichokes were sent to New York after 1904.

James Kraft ground, blended, homogenized and pasteurized cheeses for a decade to perfect the "soft packaged cheese without wasteful rind" he began selling door-to-door in Chicago in 1904. In 1915, he patented a tinned version; during World War I, the government bought more than six million tons. Afterward, Kraft sold the cheese to grocers, cut into 5-pound loaves of a perfect size for sandwiches, wrapped in foil and packed in wood boxes.

Bread and Butter Pudding

6 1/2-inch-thick slices homemade white bread
butter
ground cinnamon
ground nutmeg
1/2 cup raisins
1/2 cup chopped citron or candied orange peel
4 eggs
1/2 cup sugar
3 cups milk
1 cup cream
1 teaspoon vanilla
butter

Trim away crusts from bread and cut the slices into quarters. Butter the bread on both sides. Place half the bread in a buttered 6-cup baking dish. Sprinkle with ground cinnamon and nutmeg, raisins and citron or candied orange peel. Add the rest of the bread and a little more cinnamon. In a bowl, beat eggs with sugar until smooth. Add milk, cream and vanilla. Pour egg mixture over bread and let stand for 20 or 30 minutes. Dot the top with butter and bake in a 325°F oven for about 1 hour or until the top is crisp and brown. Serves 6. Top, if desired, with whipped cream.

Chain Grocers

Retail grocery chains grew. Besides A&P, which had 1,726 stores in 1915, there were Grand Union, Kroger Grocery and Baking Company, National Tea Company and Jewel Tea Company, to name a handful. To offer prices and a wide selection, chains dealt only in mass-produced items. Local fruits or cheeses, however splendid, were ignored.

Neighborhood grocers justified higher prices with more service. They extended credit, delivered foods and took phone orders. And they carried fresh local products.

At the turn of the century, grocers still sold staples from bins and jars, and produce from crates or baskets. Butchers kept sides (halves) and quarters of beef, pork and mutton in refrigerated storerooms and cut roasts or chops to order. Many hung poultry in the window and displayed pickled meats in barrels.

Self-Service Grocers

In September 1916, Clarence Saunders opened the first Piggly Wiggly store in Memphis. (Presumably the name derived from the nursery rhyme about "this little piggy went to market.") His store was self-service, with no counters or clerks except for selling meats. A customer entered by a turnstile, then carried a basket on a prescribed path among the shelves, putting in selections along the way. Aisles were arranged so a customer had to pass all 605 items in the store before reaching the exit where a cashier totaled the cost of the chosen items and accepted payment.

Pre-pricing items eliminated a customer's need for help, so Saunders made sales faster and cheaper than competitors could. Soon he opened other stores in the Memphis area and franchised the name—and the fixtures that ensured uniform standards—to grocers everywhere.

Obviously, Piggly Wiggly needed prepackaged foods. Crackers, for example, could not be dispensed from barrels; their baker had to weigh them and put them into cardboard or tin boxes that carried his name as well as information about their type, quality and quantity. The packaging industry grew by leaps and bounds as other stores adopted Saunders's techniques.

In 1910, Hall's pharmacy in Mifflinburg, Pennsylvania, doubled as a soda fountain serving flavored, carbonated soda waters. Developed by a druggist in Atlanta, Coca-Cola was marketed in bottles by the turn of the century.

Piggly Wiggly opened the first self-service market in Memphis in 1916 (this photo of the store was taken in 1918). Individually priced, prepackaged items eliminated the need for store clerks. The concept was franchised and soon there were dozens of Piggly Wiggly stores in the South.

Champagne Drinks

In a time of magnificent wining and dining, champagne came to be regarded as a mere ingredient. Edwardians mixed equal parts of chilled champagne and stout for a very potent potable called Black Velvet. A milder drink was made by putting a lump of sugar in a cocktail glass, adding a drop of Angostura bitters and a slice of fresh fruit (orange, lemon or peach). When the champagne was poured in, it dissolved the sugar and picked up flavor from the bitters and fruit.

Shrinking Kitchens

Increasing building costs meant a decrease in the size of kitchens at the turn of the century, and pantries were sacrificed. To compensate, cabinet makers (many located in Indiana) introduced the "Hoosier" or "Dutch" cabinet: a free-standing unit with cupboards above and below a porcelain enamel work counter. Hoosiers were such a success they soon were produced on assembly lines. Depending on size, they cost from $25 to $100. Each year, more new features were added: a spice rack, a built-in flour bin, a cutting board.

Oyster Pan Roast

The Oyster Bar in Grand Central Station in New York City, which opened in 1913, made this dish famous.

4 tablespoons butter
1 pint oysters, drained
1/2 cup chili sauce
1/2 cup heavy cream
1/2 teaspoon Worcestershire sauce

Melt butter in a skillet. Add oysters and simmer until their edges begin to curl. Stir in chili sauce, cream and Worcestershire sauce. Heat through. Season to taste. Serve at once on hot toast. Serves 4.

Gas stoves were improved enough to be considered safe by 1900, and they replaced old-fashioned wood-burners; by 1915, the ovens had thermostatically controlled temperature settings. Gas stoves not only eliminated the chores of tending a fire, but also proved easy to clean. After 1910, outer surfaces were often porcelain enamel that needed only a swipe with a dishrag. The oven was moved to a comfortable height beside the burners, and some hazard-conscious engineer designed a pilot light.

The electric stove displayed at the 1910 National Electric Light Association meeting, however, was viewed as a curiosity, perhaps due to probable cost. Electric refrigerators introduced in 1916 cost $900, which was equivalent to the average working man's annual wage.

Americans drank coffee the way the English drank tea—whenever possible. Therefore, it's no surprise that the first electric cooking appliance was a percolator introduced in 1908 by Landers, Frary and Clark. In 1909, electric toasters appeared—with exposed wires and coils. By 1910, the Westinghouse toaster-stove for "breakfast without going into the kitchen" tucked wires safely under cover. The first electric fry pan was introduced by Westinghouse in 1911; six inches across, it could be turned over

Front cover art for *The Cooking Club* magazine in March 1902 features a steaming chafing dish. Daughters of well-to-do families might attend cooking classes, learning culinary as well as household skills.

A mother teaches her daughter to cook in an illustration entitled *Her First Batch of Biscuits* that appeared in *Harper's Weekly* in 1916. Articles aimed at women included advice on child rearing, gardening, entertaining and managing the house.

for use as a hot plate, but it disappeared from the market as fast as it arrived.

For the first years of the century, a cook's biggest problem often was a power company that thought of electricity in terms of lighting and supplied it only at night. Housewives spent years persuading them to start their generators during the day.

Pots and Pans

Heavy cast-iron and flimsy tin alike were being replaced around 1900 by

Kitchen with Garland Stove, 1900—10. Wood-burning stoves were eventually replaced by coal-burning ones. Coal was more compact and easier to store, but the dust also dirtied the kitchen, requiring more cleaning.

steel cookware coated with porcelain enamel. The pots came in white with colored trim or in blue, brown, gray or black speckled agateware.

At about that time, new technology made aluminum inexpensive enough to use for cookware. (In the days of Napoleon, it was more costly than gold, and he proudly served dinner to guests on aluminum plates.) The first stamped and cast aluminum pots were made in 1892 by what is now called Alcoa; "Wear-Ever" was trademarked in 1903.

In 1913, Dr. J. T. Littleton joined the Corning Glass Works Research Laboratory. When his wife needed a cake pan in an emergency, he cut off the top of a glass laboratory battery jar (meant to withstand heat), and she used the base. It worked. Corning then spent two years perfecting the glass they dubbed Pyrex because the first product was a 9-inch pie plate.

Back in the 1880s, Charles E. Swartzbaugh, Sr., of Buffalo, New York, had introduced the Peerless Cooker—a low-pressure steam cooker with a fast-heating copper bottom—in which a housewife could cook an entire meal over one burner of a wood stove. Food burned unless the water for steaming was replenished at frequent and unpredictable intervals, but millions of cookers—some with three or four shelves inside—were sold by direct mail or door-to-door in the early 1900s.

Fare from the Fair

Affirmation of America's prosperity came from the St. Louis World's Fair of 1904. The fair also popularized two of America's most

Senator Lodge's Bean Soup

Henry Cabot Lodge, senator from Massachusetts from 1893 to 1924, gave this family recipe to the Senate Restaurant in Washington.

1 pound (2 cups) dried pea beans	2 1-pound ham hocks
water	1-1/2 cups chopped onions
1 onion pierced with 3 whole cloves	1 cup chopped celery
4 parsley sprigs	1/4 cup chopped parsley
1 bay leaf	1 teaspoon chopped garlic
2 teaspoons salt	salt and pepper

Soak beans overnight in water and cover. Drain. In a large pot, combine the beans, 2 quarts water, onion pierced with cloves, parsley sprigs, bay leaf and salt. Bring to a boil; simmer for 1 hour. (Add water if needed.) Discard the onion and herbs. Drain off the bean liquid; add water to make 3 quarts and pour it into the pot. Add ham hocks; bring to a boil; simmer for 2 hours. Stir in chopped onions, celery, parsley and garlic. Season with salt and pepper. Simmer 45 minutes. Remove the hocks; cut the ham into bite-sized pieces and add them to the soup. Serves 8 to 10.

A Sunday school picnic photographed in 1900 by Whiting Bros., finds children and adults alike attired in their Sunday-go-to-meetin' clothes. The outing undoubtedly included a variety of pies and cakes, which were commonly served at both dinner (the noon meal) and supper (the evening meal) in rural America.

enduring sandwiches: hamburgers and hot dogs.

Recipes for Hamburg steaks appear in 1800s cookbooks, but presenting the steaks on buns was a St. Louis innovation. Frankfurters or wiener-wursts had been sold in rolls at Coney Island and the New York Polo Grounds since about 1900, but St. Louis made them famous—along with R. T. French's mustard topping. (The name "hot dog" came from sports cartoonist T. A. Dorgan. In 1906, he drew lively dachs-hund-like sausages making clever comments in talk balloons.)

The story is told that English tea salesman Richard Blechtynden put ice cubes into his product at the fair to create the first glass of iced tea. Another fair first is said to be the ice cream cone. Syrian pastry-maker Ernest A. Hamwi invented it when a fellow vendor at the St. Louis Fair ran out of cups. Hamwi rolled his crisp, waffle-like zalabias into cornucopias, which not only held ice cream nicely but were edible, too. (Per capita ice cream consumption went from about one quart in 1900 to one gallon in 1915, thanks largely to cones.)

President Theodore Roosevelt, decidedly overdressed for a former cowboy, helps himself to a hearty cowboy breakfast during a visit to Colorado in 1903. Before being elected president, Roosevelt bought a partnership in a ranch, running cattle in the short-grass prairie of North Dakota.

Ethnic Foods

Between 1880 and 1920, about twenty million immigrants poured into America. Hundreds of thousands of African-Americans from southern states went north to work in defense plants during World War I, then stayed on.

Immigrants established enclaves within cities, setting up independent food systems of grocers, butchers, fishmongers and the like. In many neighborhoods, pushcarts filled streets. Some immigrants imported food—Italian spaghetti, Greek olives, Hungarian paprika, German marzipan. Others sought truck farmers to grow old-world varieties of fruits and vegetables. Restaurants opened by immigrants were patronized chiefly by neighbors. When G. Lombardi opened a pizzeria on New York's Spring Street in 1907—the first in the New World—his patrons lived nearby.

Southern Chinese from the regions around Canton and Hong Kong arrived in America in the 1840s and 1850s to seek gold and, later, to work on railroads and in logging and mining camps where they often acted as cooks. Many stayed on the West Coast, but some traveled across the country, where they labored as laundrymen or kept restaurants—the only jobs available by law and custom. Historian Richard J. Hooker suggests those Chinese may have invented egg foo yong, which developed into the famous western or Denver omelet. The history of chop suey (Cantonese for "miscellaneous fragments") is lost, but the dish was well known in New York's Chinatown by 1900.

Despite the prejudices they met, more than sixty thousand Chinese had immigrated to America

Divinity Fudge

Candy making was an orderly entertainment for well-chaperoned teenagers. Like many kinds of fudge, this should be cooked only on a dry day.

2 egg whites	1/2 cup light corn syrup
1/2 cup water	2 cups sugar

1/2 cup chopped candied cherries or chopped nuts

Separate eggs, dropping the whites into a mixing bowl; let them come to room temperature. Reserve the yolks for another use. In a heavy saucepan, bring water and corn syrup to a boil. Stir in sugar; when it dissolves cover the pan and let the syrup cook for a few minutes over medium heat to dissolve any crystals that may have formed on the sides of the pan. Uncover the syrup and let it cook until it reaches 250° F on a candy thermometer or forms a hard ball if a drop is tested in cold water. Meanwhile, beat the egg whites until they form soft peaks. When the syrup is done, pour it slowly into the egg whites while beating them constantly. Toward the end, pour and beat faster; do not scrape the pan. Beat the divinity until it is creamy. Working quickly, stir in 1/2 cup chopped candied cherries or chopped nuts. Drop the candy by spoonfuls onto waxed paper. Store in airtight containers. Makes about 1-1/2 pounds.

Olives and Bread by Glavanis depicts a simple meal that is a Mediterranean staple. From 1880 to 1920 more than 20 million immigrants entered the United States, from European countries as well as from Asia and Latin America. Ethnic neighborhoods reflected the melting pot character of the nation.

The iceman weighs a block of ice, which sold by the pound to cool refrigerators. Ice was delivered door-to-door in a horse-drawn cart. To place an order, a housewife would put a card in her front window indicating how many pounds she needed. Photo by Frances Benjamin Johnston.

The frontispiece for a 1918 cookbook entitled *A Little Candy Book for a Little Girl,* shows a girl making fudge. Concocted in the late 1800s, fudge came from New England and was usually flavored with maple sugar. When chocolate became more readily available, that became the most popular flavor.

Using Polar Bear flour, a young girl makes homemade cookies, circa 1912. The word "cookie" probably derived from the Dutch word *koekje*, meaning little cake.

by 1870. Fewer than two hundred Japanese had come by then, but their numbers increased after the passage of the Chinese Exclusion Act in 1884. An estimated 270,000 Japanese entered the United States between 1868 and 1924 when immigration from Asia virtually stopped. Unlike the Chinese, most Japanese stayed in Hawaii and California, chiefly as farmers. They opened only a handful of restaurants and their cuisine was barely known to outsiders.

Jewish immigrants to New York around the turn of the century started delicatessens (from the German word for delicacy). They dispensed bagels, lox, pastrami, Kosher pickles and cheesecake plus thick salami sandwiches and franks with sauerkraut. Delis catered chiefly to fellow immigrants except for a handful located near Broadway theaters for the convenience of Jewish performers like Eddie Cantor.

Delicatessens and "foreign" restaurants had little effect on mainstream American taste. Visiting them was considered an adventure because of the exotic food: smoked duck, bean sprouts, pastrami, pita bread. Excepted, of course, were the so-called Continental restaurants that served English, French and German dishes that had been popular in most big cities since the Revolution.

Pure Food

Tricky ways to adulterate food were ages old. Ancient Egyptians watered down beer; Greeks stretched flour with chalk. In her 1796 *American Cookery,* Amelia Simmons warned against cheese colored with "hemlock cocumberries" and fish moistened with blood to make them appear fresh. In 1900, bad eggs still were deodorized with formaldehyde for use in cakes, and jelly was produced from rotten apples. England enacted food and drug laws in 1860 and 1870, but in 1885, Nebraska Congressman A. S. Paddock was laughed at when he proposed a pure-food bill.

The drive for federal regulation of foods was led by Dr. Harvey Washington Wiley, appointed the first chief of the Bureau of Chemistry of the Department of Agriculture in 1883. He lectured widely, enlisting women's clubs' support. In 1902, he appointed a poison squad to study preservatives and colorings.

The country's leading magazines took up his causes and began attacks on filthy and adulterated foods and beverages. *The Ladies' Home Journal* and *Collier's Weekly* boosted circulation with muckraking exposes based mainly on Wiley's research. The most inflammatory work was Upton Sinclair's 1906 *The Jungle*, a novel about difficulties faced by Chicago stockyard workers. The nation was horrified by details Sinclair supplied about meat packing practices—filth, rats, sick animals passed as healthy, chopped tripe dyed red to sell as minced ham, moldy meat in sausages, even occasional humans falling victim to grinding machinery or boiling vats of lard. Sinclair himself was surprised by the uproar his novel generated. As he put it, "I aimed at the public's heart and by accident I hit it in the stomach."

That year, popular outcry pushed Congress into passing both a Meat Inspection Act and a Pure Food and Drug Act, which regulated additives and called for full ingredient labeling. Giant processors tried to turn the rules to advantage, advertising the purity of their products and opening factories to visitors—which H. J. Heinz had done for years. Even slaughterhouses held public tours.

Meat and dairy inspections were a success, in time eradicating animal diseases like tuberculosis; yet enforcing the new legislation was problematic. Despite Wiley's protest, the dried fruit industry got permission to treat their product with sulfur. Millers went on bleaching flour. In 1912, a discouraged Wiley resigned.

Although other reforms slowed, pasteurization laws passed city by city, state by state. The milk bottle Dr. Harvey D. Thatcher invented in 1884 was improved and mass produced, eliminating the need to dip portions from ten-gallon tin cans and making the milk supply even safer.

Eggs à la Goldenrod

A perfect dainty for ladies' luncheons:

4 eggs	1 cup milk
1 tablespoon butter	salt and white pepper
1 tablespoon flour	4 slices white bread, toasted

Hard-boil eggs. Cool and peel them; separate the whites from the yolks. Make a thin white sauce: Melt butter in medium saucepan. Stir in flour. Gradually whisk in milk and cook until slightly thickened. Season with salt and ground white pepper. Mince egg whites and add them to the sauce. Cut toasted bread slices lengthwise into halves or thirds. Arrange them on a platter and pour the sauce over them. Force the yolks through a ricer or strainer to decorate the top. Garnish with fresh parsley sprigs. Serves 4.

An illustration by Edward Penfield for *Pure Food Campaigns*, 1913. Popular since the mid-1800s, when the airtight mason jar was invented, home canning remained important for rural homemakers, who preserved fruits and vegetables from their summer gardens to eat all year long.

Nutrition

During the 1800s, the science of nutrition was born when Sir Edward Frankland in London began analysis of food's energy—or calorie—value. By 1900, nutritionists taught that food consisted of carbonaceous or heat-producing elements and nitrogenous or muscle-building elements. Fats and carbohydrates furnished energy and heat; proteins built and repaired tissue.

In 1911, the Polish chemist Casimir Funk isolated a water-soluble nutrient he believed was an amine. He prefixed that word with *vita*, Latin for life, and coined "vitamine." Later the "e" was dropped, and Funk's nutrient classified as Vitamin B-1. In 1913, E. V. McCollum and M. Davis at Yale isolated fat-soluble Vitamin A and showed that a lack of it stunted growth and caused poor vision. (Colleagues found a rich source of A was cod liver oil—soon the bane of children.)

Stuffed turkey was the traditional meal served at Thanksgiving and Christmas. It was also tradition for the father to carve the bird, as seen here in a 1936 illustration entitled *The Long Table Quite Full* by Thomas Fogarty.

Food for World War I

When the United States entered World War I on April 6, 1917, it had to feed not only its citizens and armed forces, but also its allies. President Woodrow Wilson created the United States Food Administration and named Herbert Hoover, who had directed food distribution in war-torn Belgium and northern France, to head it.

The USFA used schools, pulpits, posters, newspapers and motion pictures to make food-saving a national priority. It explained calories, vitamins, and proteins, and taught food preservation. It told the public that "Food Will Win the War" if they practiced the "Gospel of the Clean Plate." Hoover promoted whole cereals and fresh fruits and vegetables, particularly potatoes and beans. Families were urged to plant vegetables in their backyards, in what came to be called Liberty Gardens.

Fruit Jelly

3 pounds of fruit, to yield about 4 cups of juice (no pineapple or quince)

3/4 cup sugar for each cup of juice

Equipment:

Large saucepan
Colander
Cheesecloth
Jars
Paraffin

Small saucepan
2 large bowls
Teakettle full of water
Hot pad mittens
(to lift jars of hot water)

Wash the fruit and cut into small pieces. (Do not peel or core.) Put fruit in saucepan and cook until it creates juice, in about 5 to 15 minutes. If necessary, add some water to keep fruit from burning. Strain fruit through a colander into a bowl. Wash colander and place it over the second large bowl. Pour the juice from the first bowl through several layers of cheesecloth draped over the colander. Let the juice drip through for about an hour. Measure juice by the cup into the saucepan. Boil juice for 5 minutes. Add 3/4 cup of sugar for each cup of fruit juice. Boil mixture for 15 to 30 minutes or until mixture jells or thickens. Test to see if it has jelled by putting a few drops in the freezer for a few minutes to see if it gets thick when cooled. Boil water in the teakettle. Pour boiling water into jars, and then immediately empty the jars and fill with jelly. Melt paraffin in a small saucepan over very low heat. Pour about 1/2 inch of melted paraffin over the top of each jar of jelly. Let it cool. Jars are now sealed and can be stored in a cool, dry place.

In January 1918, Hoover asked for wheatless Mondays and Wednesdays, meatless Tuesdays, porkless Thursdays and Saturdays and victory bread, high in bran. He raised wheat prices, encouraging farmers to increase crops.

Margarine had been available since the 1880s, but only wartime butter shortages induced families to try it. This was because a 1902 tax inflated the price of yellow-tinted margarine. The frugal housewife who bought the unappealing white version had to mix it with coloring material to produce a buttery-looking spread.

The war also led cooks to try Crisco, America's first hydrogenated shortening. (Adding hydrogen made vegetable oil partially solid; when heated, hydrogen escaped and the oil became fluid again.) Crisco was introduced by Procter & Gamble in 1911. It did not go rancid, and it withstood the high heat of frying, but because it came from a soap company, cooks worried. Not until lard got scarce in 1917 did Crisco sales soar.

FOOD WILL WIN THE WAR
You came here seeking Freedom
You must now help to preserve it

WHEAT is needed for the allies
Waste nothing

UNITED STATES FOOD ADMINISTRATION

This U.S. Food Administration poster calls on American patriotism to aid in the war effort during World War I. Wheat was needed to feed allied troops. In 1918, then head of the U.S. Food Administration, Herbert Hoover asked citizens to observe wheatless Mondays and Wednesdays.

An illustration of strawberry shortcake as it appeared in *War Time Recipes,* by Janet Hill, 1918.

Chapter Five
The Jazz Age (1920–1930)

*D*rink seemed a lot more interesting than food in the "Roaring Twenties." It certainly grabbed more headlines with bootleggers and speakeasies spawned by the Noble Experiment of Prohibition—the Eighteenth Amendment that went into effect January 16, 1920. The decade ended on a sober note, however, when the Stock Market crashed. On Black Tuesday, October 29, 1929, the Great Depression began.

"DIGGING IN" IN AMERICA. . . .BY "BART".

NOW DON'T ANYBODY WAIT!

With the war in Europe over, foods were no longer rationed and an era of prosperity prevailed. This cartoon by Charles L. Bartholomew shows plenty to go around and everyone "digging in."

Uniform Cookery

The 1924 National Origins Act had cut immigration and an already dwindling supply of domestic help. The newly enfranchised housewife had no choice but to cook. She probably knew the basics but rarely was encouraged to apply them with imagination. The Smith-Hughes Act of 1917 funded high school instruction in domestic arts, now generally called home economics, where teachers stressed standardized and scientific—not creative—cookery.

Furthermore, like as not, a housewife's recipes came from women's magazines, syndicated newspaper columns or food manufacturers—all national sources. Regional foods disappeared while cooks across the country tried to fix identical versions of stews, soups, soufflés and such. Processed foods, another force for uniformity, became staples.

Elaborate dinner parties were becoming passé. When families entertained, serving canned or packaged products was no embarrassment. The ladies' mah-jongg club might share a main-course salad of canned cut-up fruits and marshmallow bits, embedded in a flavored gelatin mold and presented with dabs of sweet grocery-store mayonnaise. In the evening, couples met to dance to Victrola or radio music, play bridge and drink bootleg whiskey or enjoy a simple sweet like pineapple upside-down cake. (Canned pineapple was the food fad of 1923.)

The only enthusiastic cook seemed to be Betty Crocker.

Swiss Steak

According to food historian John Mariani, the term Swiss Steak first appeared in print in 1924. Since then variations have multiplied.

> 1/2 cup flour
> salt and pepper
> 2-pound boneless round steak, 1 inch thick
> 2 tablespoons bacon drippings or oil
> 2 onions, thinly sliced
> beef stock, milk or cream

Season flour generously with salt and pepper, and use a meat mallet to pound as much flour as possible into both sides of the round steak. Gash the edges of the steak to prevent curling. Sear the steak on both sides in bacon drippings or oil in a heavy casserole. Transfer the steak to a plate, stir onions into the fat remaining in the casserole. When they are soft, return the steak and add enough beef stock to immerse the meat halfway. Cover and bake at 350°F for 1 hour or until the steak is tender. Pour off the cooking liquid, skim the fat from its surface and return 2 tablespoons of the fat to the casserole; add 2 tablespoons flour. Over high heat, whisk in the reserved cooking liquid to make pan gravy. Add beef stock, milk or cream, as needed. Season to taste. Pour the gravy over the steak. Serve with boiled or mashed potatoes. Serves 4–6.

Shelves are stacked high with canned and packaged goods in a Washington, D.C., grocery store circa 1920. Processed foods brought a uniformity to the American diet, as did the proliferation of recipes published in nationally distributed magazines, factors that added to the decline of regional cooking styles.

Eggs Benedict

It's said this dish was created at Delmonico's restaurant in New York City for a patron whose surname was Benedict.

1 English muffin
2 slices Canadian bacon
2 tablespoons butter
2 eggs
hollandaise sauce
truffle or ripe olive

Split and toast English muffin. Sauté Canadian bacon in butter and poach the eggs. When the bacon browns, put a slice on each muffin half and top with a poached egg. Pour hollandaise sauce over all. Decorate each egg with a tiny piece of truffle (or ripe olive). Serve at once. Serves 1.

In 1921, Washburn Crosby Company (part of General Mills after 1928) promoted Gold Medal flour with a picture puzzle contest in a national magazine. When entrants asked baking questions, the company created "Betty Crocker" to sign answers to the mail. They chose the name "Betty" for folksiness; "Crocker" honored a former company director. At first, Betty was only a signature. But in 1924, she became a radio voice on the "Betty Crocker Cooking School of the Air," broadcast from thirteen regional stations by actresses with appropriate accents.

Kitchenettes

As interest in cooking waned, the kitchen shrank. In the city apartment, it was small enough to go by the modish name of "kitchenette." The maid's room disappeared when architects discovered appliances often could replace the hired girl.

Certainly sales of appliances boomed. An electric mixer was mounted on a stand. An electric sandwich toaster and waffle iron "for lamp socket use" were introduced. The flip-flop toaster that turned over a slice of bread by lowering a side panel came onto the market. In 1927, Toastmaster showed a pop-up toaster.

By 1922, the Hoosier cupboard was outmoded by cabinets that could be arranged in various ways. Porcelain work surfaces had been so popular that manufacturers put them on wood tables, some with drawers and bins under the slick tops.

An up-to-date kitchen had a linoleum rug or, fancier yet, "inlaid" linoleum (meaning permanently installed from wall to wall). White gas stoves were prized in cities and suburbs alike. In homes beyond city gas lines, customers used bottled gas, actually metal tanks of liquid propane or "l.p."

Iceboxes were still popular because refrigerators were expensive. By the 1920s, these were enamel-coated porcelain. General Electric's famous "Monitor Top" version had exposed coils above the box. Whatever the maker, a capacity

Upside Down Cake

1/4 cup butter	4 eggs, separated
1 cup brown sugar	1 tablespoon canned fruit juice
canned pineapple rings or	1 teaspoon vanilla
canned sliced peaches	1 cup sugar
maraschino cherries or	1 cup cake flour
walnut halves	1 teaspoon baking powder

Melt butter in a large, heavy ovenproof skillet. Add brown sugar and stir until it dissolves. Off the heat, arrange canned pineapple rings or canned sliced peaches on the sugary caramel. Center a maraschino cherry in each pineapple ring or set walnut halves around the peach slices. Make a cake batter by first beating egg yolks until smooth. Stir in canned fruit juice and vanilla extract. Beat egg whites until stiff, slowly fold in sugar, then gradually add the yolk mixture and incorporate cake flour that has been sifted with baking powder. Pour the batter over the fruit. Bake at 350°F for 20 to 30 minutes or until a toothpick inserted into the cake comes out clean. Immediately cover the skillet with a serving plate. Remembering that the butter-sugar caramel may be hotter than boiling, quickly—but cautiously—invert the skillet and plate together. Leave the skillet in place for a few minutes before carefully lifting it off.

Instructors from the United States Department of Agriculture Extension Service teach rural housewives cooking skills circa 1925. The government now took an interest in making foods healthier and safer. The Pure Food and Drug Act was enacted in 1906 along with the Meat Inspection Act.

of 5 or 6 cubic feet was common. (Today's average is about 18 feet.)

New Foods

Broccoli—often called Italian asparagus—had been grown in American gardens since the early 1700s, but wasn't widely known until two centuries later when New York farmers began shipping it west and south in the 1920s. Artichokes were shipped east from California, and avocados went north from Florida.

Cranberry Orange Sauce

1/2 pound (2 cups) fresh cranberries
1 cup sugar
1/2 cup water
1 tablespoon grated orange peel

Wash cranberries and put in glass, enameled or stainless steel saucepan with sugar and water. Stirring, bring to a boil over high heat. Reduce heat and simmer for about 5 minutes or until berry skins begin to pop. Remove from heat and stir in grated orange peel. Pour into small bowl or 2-cup mold. Refrigerate 3 hours or until sauce feels firm when touched. Unmold it onto a serving plate.

In 1921, Taggart Baking Company of Indianapolis introduced Wonder Bread—its wrappers decorated with multicolor balloons inspired by an International Balloon Race at the Indianapolis Speedway. In 1925, Continental bought Taggart and Wonder became a national brand.

Sanka appeared in America in 1923, a harbinger of what eventually became a shelf full of decaffeinated coffees. Sanka owed its existence to a 1903 storm that soaked coffee beans bound for Dr. Ludwig Roselius's firm in Bremen, Germany. He gave the brine-ruined beans to researchers for

Green Goddess Dressing

This dressing was created at San Francisco's Palace Hotel in the mid-1920s for the English actor George Arliss who was in town, starring in a play called *The Green Goddess*.

 1 cup mayonnaise
 3 anchovy fillets, minced
 1 tablespoon finely cut fresh chives
 1 teaspoon minced fresh tarragon (or 1/2 teaspoon dried)
 1 teaspoon tarragon vinegar

In a bowl, combine mayonnaise with anchovy fillets, parsley, chives, tarragon and vinegar. Use as a dressing for chicken, fish or shellfish.

his pet project: taking caffeine out of coffee. Tests led to a process that removed 97 percent of coffee's caffeine. Roselius introduced his product in France (Sanka is a contraction of *sans caffeine*) just before World War I.

Ice Cream

The soda fountain was the center of teen-age social life. Its soda jerk presided over a battery of ice creams, sauces, syrups for drinks such as Coca-Cola and Dr. Pepper, soda water and crushed ice.

In 1921, Christian Nelson, who owned an ice cream parlor in Onawa, Iowa, teamed up with marketer Russell Stover to sell his Eskimo Pie—a slice of ice cream coated with chocolate and wrapped in aluminum foil. Stover took the pie national then moved to Denver and used his fee from Nelson to start a chain of candy stores.

The Eskimo Pie was hand-held and tricky to eat before it melted. Harry B. Burt, Sr. of Youngstown, Ohio, solved that problem in 1923 by putting the ice cream on a stick before dipping it in

This simple rural kitchen photographed in the late 1920s is homey and comfortable, an important quality for the room of the house in which the women spent most of their time.

"There is something so cheery and friendly about a pretty kitchen," reads the advertising copy for Congoleum Art Rugs. "No more wasting your strength and time in sweeping and beating old-fashioned, woven floor-coverings. No more cleaning-day fatigue." This ad for the Congoleum Rug appeared in *Better Homes and Gardens* while the two-page ad [at bottom] ran in *Literary Digest*—a reflection of the diverse interests of women in the 1920s.

Items on these shelves photographed in the late 1920s bear national brand names still familiar today, such as Jell-O, Minute Tapioca, Baker's Coconut and Royal Food Coloring.

Cold Refreshing
ready at any time with Frigidaire

Always plenty of ice cubes

WHAT a comfort on hot days to have a generous-sized bowl kept full of ice cubes—and to have a never-failing source that keeps the supply constantly replenished!

That's just one of the delights of Frigidaire electric refrigeration. And, no matter how many pounds of ice you take from Frigidaire, the food compartment is always cold—always safe for the preservation of even the most perishable meats and vegetables.

Then, too, you can prepare many new and tempting dishes in the Frigidaire freezing compartment. And you know a new freedom.

Freedom from outside ice supply—more time away from the kitchen —more leisure hours.

Begin now to enjoy the new comfort and convenience of Frigidaire. Remember that Frigidaire is the name of the electric refrigerator that offers you all these advantages:

(1) Complete and permanent independence of outside ice supply.

(2) Uninterrupted service—proved by the experience of more than 300,000 users—more than all other electric refrigerators combined.

(3) A food compartment that is 12° colder than you can expect with ice—temperatures that keep foods fresh.

(4) Direct frost-coil cooling and self-sealing tray fronts, giving a dessert and ice-making compartment *always below freezing.*

(5) Beautiful metal cabinets designed, built and insulated exclusively for electric refrigeration.

(6) An operating cost that is surprisingly low.

(7) Value only made possible by quantity production, General Motors purchasing power and G.M.A.C. terms.

Write to us for complete information about Frigidaire, or visit the nearest Frigidaire Sales Office.

FRIGIDAIRE CORPORATION
Subsidiary of General Motors Corporation
Dept. A-121   Dayton, Ohio

Even the smallest Frigidaire makes 5 pounds of ice cubes between meals —always plenty.

Frigidaire
PRODUCT of GENERAL MOTORS

In using advertisements see page 6   125

Ad in *Good Housekeeping,* July 1927. The electric Frigidaire was equipped with a freezer compartment. General Electric promoted its "complete and permanent independence of outside ice supply," which left the housewife more time to play tennis or pursue other leisure activities.

chocolate, then packing it in salted ice to harden the coating. He sold this Good Humor Ice Cream Sucker from his candy shop until inspired to paint a refrigerated truck white, put bells on it and hire a white-coated driver to go around town selling ice cream. The truck was the forerunner of what became fleets of Good Humor trucks.

The next year, Frank Epperson, who ran a lemonade stand at an amusement park in Oakland, California, decided to patent the Epsicle or Popsicle, which he had invented accidentally as a child by freezing a stick in a mixture of soda pop powder and water. Burt complained that this product infringed on his Good Humor. They compromised when Epperson agreed to make just water-ice products while Burt used just ice cream.

Spanish Rice

Any dish containing pimiento seemed Spanish—and exotic.

> 4 bacon slices, minced
> 1/2 cup rice
> 1 onion, chopped
> 1 green pepper, chopped
> 1-1/2 cups canned tomato pieces with juice
> 1 diced pimiento
> water

Sauté the bacon slices in an ovenproof skillet; when crisp, remove the bacon. Stir rice into the bacon fat. Add onion and green pepper. Sauté until the onion is soft. Add canned tomato pieces with their juice, the sautéed bacon and pimiento. Bake covered at 325°F for 30 minutes. Add water if the rice gets too dry. Serves 4.

At this soda fountain on Long Island, the soda jerk made drinks by squirting flavored syrup into a glass and adding carbonated soda water. Eggs and cream were also added. Reportedly the ice cream soda was invented when a concessionaire in Philadelphia, having run out of cream, added a scoop of vanilla ice cream as a substitute, hoping no one would notice the difference.

Customers line up for cold apple cider at a roadside stand, circa 1929. Refreshing and healthful, sweet cider was made by squeezing fruit pulp through a press to extract the juice. Temperance leaders railed against fermented hard cider, and fanatics were known to have chopped down entire apple orchards.

This debutante dinner took place in the elegant Willard Hotel in Washington, D.C., in 1920, just days before Prohibition would go into effect outlawing alcoholic beverages. While there are no cocktails evident on this elaborately decorated table, flasks were probably slipped into pockets and purses.

The Eighteenth Amendment prohibited drinking, but many found ways around the law, such as this woman with a hollowed out cane for dispensing hooch.

Prohibition

With Prohibition, American wineries closed except for those licensed to produce wines for medical or religious purposes. Wealthy Americans had laid in substantial stocks of fine wines and spirits. But most drinkers experimented with home brews and bathtub gin, or patronized speakeasies (illegal saloons) often operated by mobsters and supplied by rum-runners or—in the southern states—by "stillers."

Ironically, Prohibition gave whiskey cachet. Before 1920, only about a third of all alcoholic drinks held hard liquor. By 1930, three-fourths did. Cocktails made the switch nearly painless. The cocktail is an American invention, the story goes, named by a Revolutionary War soldier for the feather or "cock's tail" decorating a rum-and-fruit drink. In fact, mixed drinks were popular from Colonial times when spirits needed sweetening to be palatable. Prohibition continued that tradition, forcing the drinker to choose between pallid "near beer" and a mixed drink. Sweet sodas found a new market, and their sales surged.

Apple Pandowdy

Some cooks call this Apple Jonathan. The "dowdy" in the name presumably suggests its simplicity.

6 apples	1/2 teaspoon ginger
1 cup light molasses	1/4 teaspoon cloves
1 teaspoon cinnamon	prepared pie pastry
1 teaspoon nutmeg	heavy cream

Peel, core and slice apples. Arrange the slices in a 9-inch square baking dish. Combine molasses with cinnamon, nutmeg, ginger and cloves. Drizzle the mixture over the apples. Cover the top with pie pastry. Slit the pastry in two or three places. Bake at 350°F for 1 hour or until the pastry is well browned. Serve warm, crust-side down, accompanied by heavy cream.

Roadside stands like this one photographed in the mid-1920s were common in rural areas. The farmer or farmer's wife sold fresh fruits and vegetables, or even baked goods, to people driving by.

Scalloped Oysters

Every New England family had a version of this recipe. Some added grated nutmeg, others added a spoonful of dry sherry. Milk was often substituted for the cream.

1 cup fine cracker crumbs	2 tablespoons heavy cream
1/2 cup bread crumbs	salt and pepper
1/2 cup melted butter	butter
1 pint freshly shucked oysters, reserve 1/4 cup liquor	

Combine cracker crumbs with bread crumbs. Stir in melted butter. Spread a layer of crumbs in a deep 8-inch pie dish, using about one-third of them. Drain oysters; reserve 1/4 cup of their liquor and mix it with heavy cream. Lay half of the oysters over the crumbs, pour in half of the liquid mixture; season with salt and pepper. Cover with a layer of crumbs, then the remaining oysters and liquor. Top with the rest of the crumbs and dots of butter. Bake at 450°F for 20 minutes or until the liquid bubbles and the crumbs are golden brown. Serves 4.

Cocktail parties were now stylish home entertainment. Accompanying the drinks was a new category of comestible: "finger food" that could be held in the fingers and eaten in a bite or two without the aid of forks or spoons.

Nutrition and Health

In 1920, J. C. Drummond identified Vitamin C. In 1922, McCollum and Davis isolated Vitamin D and showed its relationship to rickets. Scientists found that B was a mixture of nutrients and discovered the importance of dietary iron in preventing anemia. And in 1928, chemists at the University of Wisconsin irradiated pasteurized milk with vitamin D—a nutrient it had never had.

Women fill jars of peanut butter, which was invented by a St. Louis doctor in 1890 and extolled for its nutritive value.

As links were established between vitamins and good health, public interest grew. When it was found that lack of food iodine caused goiters (enlargements of the thyroid gland) among Midwesterners, the Michigan Medical Association asked Morton Salt to iodize their product and give consumers a simple source for this nutrient. To get necessary iron for her family, a housewife cooked liver (with onions or bacon, probably) on a regular basis.

Stewed Tomatoes

3 cups drained canned tomatoes	1/2 cup soft bread crumbs
4 tablespoons brown sugar	enough 1-inch bread squares
1 teaspoon salt	to top baking dish
black pepper	2 tablespoons butter

Combine tomatoes with 2 tablespoons brown sugar, salt and a grinding of black pepper. Butter a small baking dish and sprinkle in bread crumbs. Add the tomato mixture and top with 1-inch bread squares. Dot with butter cut into tiny pieces, and sprinkle with remaining 2 tablespoons brown sugar. Bake at 400°F until brown and bubbly. Serves 4.

After tomatoes and grapefruit were identified as rich in Vitamin C, food processors rushed to can their juice.

By the mid-1920s, kitchen sinks like this one were made of white porcelain enamel, a surface that could be easily cleaned with a wet rag. Soon other kitchen appliances were also made of enamel.

Chapter Six
The Lean Years (1930–1940)

*A*fter the stock market crashed, frugality became a mandate for cooks. Factories and stores started closing in 1930; millions of people found themselves out of work. When Pacific apple growers harvested a surplus that year, unemployed men and women sold the fruit for a nickel apiece on city streets nationwide. New York alone had six thousand apple peddlers. The business was as short-lived as the surplus but came to symbolize the Great Depression in America.

For this man in Nicholson Hollow, Virginia, in 1935, selling a bushel of apples might mean the difference between feeding his family—or not. During the Great Depression people throughout the nation were out of work, and unemployment ran as high as 25 percent. People in the Appalachian Mountains, poor even before the depression, were particularly hard hit.

The Farm Security Administration, part of President Franklin D. Roosevelt's New Deal, put writers and photographers to work documenting rural life in the United States. This 1936 photograph by Walker Evans, who became well known for his work for the FSA, shows a roadside stand in Louisiana advertising poor boy sandwiches.

The Salvation Army, hospitals, churches and fraternal orders kept breadlines and soup kitchens open year-round. Begging increased; thievery rose. During January 1931, food riots took place in Arkansas and Oklahoma. In March 1933, when Franklin D. Roosevelt was inaugurated president, unemployment exceeded 25 percent. The government spent billions of dollars on thousands of work projects during the following years, but full employment seemed unattainable because the depression was global. In Europe, it contributed to the rise of Hitler and —at the decade's end—to World War II.

Everyday Dinner

Essayist E. B. White understood: "The vision of milk and honey, it comes and goes. But the odor of cooking goes on forever." Depression or no, food was the best cure for low spirits, and cooks outdid themselves to invent and uplift.

Women were sent home as existing jobs went to men. Articles in magazines and newspapers agreed that woman's place was in the kitchen. Gathering the family together at dinnertime was the secret to success in marriage and in raising children. Cans and boxes filled kitchen cabinets as consumption of commercially processed fruits and vegetables rose by 50 percent. Even the poor wanted canned goods; brand-name food had status.

Wealthy families who managed to keep their money ate better than ever, waited on by a retinue of newly affordable servants. Their food was French or French-ified: *filets de sole, côtes de veau, tournedos à la sauce Bearnaise, gâteau Saint-Honoré.*

The working class did not share the sole, veal cutlets, tenderloin steaks or cream puffs. For them, Sundays and holidays were generally marked by simple roasted meat or chicken with mashed potatoes and gravy, fruit pie or layer cake. Thanks to the home food grinder, leftovers translated into hashes or savory pies for weekdays. In a ham loaf, bread crumbs stretched a few scraps of meat into a meal for six.

Macaroni and Cheese

8 ounces elbow macaroni
8 ounces grated Cheddar cheese (about 2 cups after grating)
2 tablespoons butter
2 tablespoons flour
1-1/2 cups milk
salt and pepper

Boil and drain elbow macaroni. In a buttered baking dish, mix macaroni with 6 ounces grated Cheddar cheese (about 1-1/2 cups). Make a cream sauce: Melt butter in a medium saucepan, stir in flour; gradually whisk in milk. Cook until thickened. Season with salt and pepper. Pour the cream sauce over the macaroni. Sprinkle 2 ounces grated Cheddar (about 1/2 cup) on top. Bake at 350°F for 30 minutes or until the sauce is absorbed and the topping melted to a golden crust. Serves 2–4.

Americans had always preferred meat-and-potatoes menus. Now cooks learned to extend meat in casseroles that consisted chiefly of starch: scalloped potatoes and ham, shepherd's pie with mashed potatoes and stewed meat. Casseroles not only simplified cooking, but also could utilize cheap cuts of meat since ingredients were chopped or sliced thin.

For many Americans, casseroles represented the first "foreign" food at the family table. European cuisines were rich in such dishes: *lasagne, cassoulet, goulash, moussaka, arroz con pollo.* American versions of these classics were tame, with little seasoning or

The Farm Security Administration also worked directly with rural families. This 1939 photograph by Arthur Rothstein, taken in Missouri, is captioned "The FSA county home supervisor is helping Mrs. Dixon to plan a practiced way of managing her household." With smiles all around, it seemed to be working.

Scalloped Potatoes with Ham

4 cups peeled, thinly
  sliced potatoes
2 cups bite-sized pieces
  baked or boiled ham
4 tablespoons butter
3 tablespoons flour

2 cups milk
1 teaspoon dry mustard
1 teaspoon salt
1/4 teaspoon red pepper
2 cups shredded Cheddar
  cheese (about 1/2 pound)

Butter an 8-to10-cup casserole. Prepare potatoes and ham. In a sauce-pan, melt butter; whisk in flour, then milk; boil, then cook over low heat for 3 or 4 minutes. Season with dry mustard, salt and red pepper. Stir in Cheddar cheese. Place a layer of potatoes in the casserole, add a layer of ham; repeat, ending with potatoes. Pour the cheese sauce over the top. Cover with a lid or foil. Bake at 350°F for 45 minutes, then uncover and bake 15 minutes longer to brown the top. Serves 6.

In 1935, canning fruit was women's work in Oklahoma, where wheat farms stretched to the horizons. When unsound farming practices left topsoil subject to erosion, farmlands literally blew away. Thrown into poverty and unable to feed their families, thousands left the state during the Dust Bowl days of the 1930s. As immortalized in John Steinbeck's *The Grapes of Wrath,* many "Okies" became migrant workers in other states, picking crops for just pennies.

spice. By and large, when foods with foreign names were served, only the words were exotic. Chili con carne, for example, held mostly beans and tomatoes with a little beef and a trace of chili powder. Bechamel sauce, enriched by just enough curry powder to turn it from white to yellow, upgraded halved hard-cooked eggs into a main course. Veal goulash with no paprika was sauced with sweet bottled chili sauce. And Americans also invented "foreign" treats—spaghetti with meatballs, Swiss steak, Russian dressing.

Ground beef, once reserved chiefly for meatballs, soared in popularity. Sarah Tyson Rorer had published the first American meatloaf recipe in her 1902 cookbook, and about the same time, Dr. J. H. Salisbury was recommending broiled ground beef patties eaten three times a day as a cure for ailments ranging from gout to asthma. During the depression, meatloaf and Salisbury steak (often smothered by canned mushroom soup) became dinner standards because the price was right.

Convenience Foods

A clever Pullman dining-car chef invented Bisquick—a mix of flour, leavening and lard that he stocked in his refrigerator so he could make biscuit dough quickly by just adding milk. A General Mills salesman took the idea to that company's chemist, Charles Kress, who found shortening (sesame oil, originally) that would not turn rancid. Bisquick debuted in 1930.

Another timesaver was presliced bread introduced in 1930 by Wonder to a first suspicious, then delighted, national market—that memorialized the occasion with the expression "the greatest thing since sliced bread." Both packaged macaroni and cheese from Kraft and the canned, ready-to-eat spiced ham called Spam, appeared in 1937.

Children in Kentucky in 1940 take off from school for "syrupping off" days in early fall, when cane is boiled down into sorghum syrup. A neighbor oversees the process, doing the work for other members of the community and taking a share of the syrup for his labor. Photo by Marion Post Wolcott.

The original supermarket, A&P advertised self-service and low prices. By buying in volume, chain stores could sell for much less than local grocery stores. Photo by Jack Delano for the Farm Security Administration, Durham, North Carolina, 1940.

Beans and Franks

2 slices bacon, chopped
1 small onion, chopped
1 No. 3 can pork and beans
   (about 3-1/2 cups)

1/4 cup brown sugar
1 tablespoon prepared mustard
6 frankfurters, sliced

In a heavy saucepan, sauté bacon until crispy. Remove and drain the bacon; sauté onion in the fat remaining in the pan. When the onion is soft and golden, add pork and beans (about 3-1/2 cups), brown sugar, prepared mustard, and frankfurters. Mix well, cover and simmer for about 20 minutes. Serves 6.

Corn Oysters

2 eggs
1/2 cup flour
1/2 teaspoon baking powder
1/2 teaspoon salt
nutmeg

1 cup cooked corn
2 tablespoons bacon drippings
   or butter
maple syrup

In a bowl, beat eggs until smooth. Add flour, baking powder, salt and an ample grating of nutmeg. Stir in corn, freshly scraped from cobs or drained well if canned. Melt bacon drippings or butter on a griddle or in a heavy skillet. Drop the corn batter by the tablespoonful onto the griddle. Brown these "oysters" on both sides. Serve at once with maple syrup. Serves 2 or 3.

Cole Slaw with Boiled Salad Dressing

2 tablespoons flour
1 tablespoon sugar
1 teaspoon dry mustard
1/2 teaspoon paprika
1/2 teaspoon salt
1/2 cup milk

2 egg yolks
1/4 cup vinegar
1 small head cabbage
1 carrot, finely chopped
1/2 cup chopped green pepper
1/2 cup chopped onion (optional)

In a small bowl, mix together flour, sugar, dry mustard, paprika and salt. Stir in milk. In the top of a double boiler over—not in—boiling water, beat egg yolks until pale. Stir in vinegar, then add the milk mixture. Cook and stir until the dressing is thick and smooth. Set the dressing aside to cool. Remove the outer leaves from cabbage. Quarter it, cut out the core, and cut the rest into thin shreds. In a serving bowl, combine the cabbage with carrot, green pepper and onion, if desired. Pour the boiled dressing over the vegetables and mix well.

In 1930, Ruth Wakefield who ran the Toll House Inn of Whitman, Massachusetts, cut pieces off a bar of semi-sweet chocolate to flavor cookies. The pieces softened but kept their identity in baking. Wakefield wrote Nestlé, who put a recipe for "Toll House Cookies" on their bar chocolate. Already-cut morsels, or chips (really, teardrop-shaped), followed in 1939.

Envelopes of shamelessly sweet Kool-Aid popped up in grocery stores in 1931. Originally, E. E. Perkins had sold syrup flavorings by mail from Hastings, Nebraska. When he developed a more mailable—and saleable—concentrated powder, he named it Kool-Aid Instant Soft Drink Mix and set up his headquarters in Chicago.

Cut-Rate Grocers

Chain grocery stores were entrenched nationwide. Piggly Wiggly had franchised dozens of self-help grocery stores. Then, on August 4, 1930, Michael Cullen opened a self-service super market called King Kullen in Jamaica, Long Island, in what had been an automobile garage. Eliminating frills allowed Cullen to set prices lower than competitors'. He took out newspaper ads styling himself as the World's Greatest Price Wrecker. His motto was "Why Pay More?" Cullen sold a 15-cent box of Shredded Wheat for 9 1/2 cents and a 25-cent can of Crisco for 21 cents, in a time when pennies mattered.

During the 1930s, Cullen opened almost two dozen more markets on Long Island. Plain but clean, they were located away from downtown traffic and had ample parking lots for shoppers who wanted to stock up on groceries. Although called "super markets" (later made one word), they were small by modern standards—5,000 to 10,000 square feet with about 1,100 different items. They undercut competitors, who went so far as to ask newspapers to refuse King Kullen ads. (That plan failed.) By the end of the decade, even big chains were copying Cullen.

Farm Security Administration. This 1940 photograph documents a grocery store in Lincoln, Nebraska, with oranges selling for just one cent apiece. Photo by John Vachon.

During a roundup at the Walking X cattle ranch in Texas, a cowboy dishes up a noonday meal of a beefy chili. With endless miles of range for cattle to feed, Texas became—and still is—the nation's leading producer of beef. FSA photo by Russell Lee, near Marfa, Texas, 1939.

Cookbooks and Recipes

Women were bombarded with recipe booklets from manufacturers eager to sell their wares. By the 1930s, most newspapers ran some sort of women's page with kitchen hints. Canned and boxed foods carried recipes. Appliance and utility companies employed home economist demonstrators and donated appliances to schools where home economics was increasingly important.

Woman's Day and *Family Circle* magazines began as giveaways from A&P and Safeway, respectively. *Woman's Day* originated in 1931 as a menu helper with recipes included; by 1937, it became a bona fide magazine, and a copy cost two cents. *Family Circle*, begun in 1932, consisted of 24 pages, 8 1/2 of them advertising; it was devoted to recipes and stories about celebrities because the first editor was Harry Evans, a Hollywood talent scout.

Appropriately, cookbooks stressed thrift. *The Most for Your Money* gave recipes for making calves' hearts—two for a dime then—into "ritzy dishes we wouldn't be ashamed to set before Oscar at the Waldorf."

That cookbook paradigm—*The Joy of Cooking* by Irma Starkloff Rombauer, a St. Louis socialite—was privately printed in 1931. Although she introduced it as "a compilation of reliable recipes with casual culinary notes," the 395-page volume, illustrated by her daughter Marion Rombauer Becker, was both authoritative and ambitious. In 1936, Bobbs-Merrill Company published a 628-page version, still written in the personal style that made Rombauer seem an old friend to her readers.

In 1930, the original 210-page *Better Homes & Gardens Cookbook* appeared in a blue-ring binder, and the 256-page *Good Housekeeping Cook Book* was published. Both classics-to-be stressed simple, hardy foods: pot roast, pork chops with apple sauce, peach cobbler. Even when Prohibition was repealed, the books—and magazines—avoided wine, beer or anything stronger in recipes and menus lest they offend readers who thought rum was a demon.

A familiar sight and sound to children throughout the country, the Good Humor man sold ice cream bars and Popsicles on a stick. Photographed in Alexandria, Virginia, in 1941, these sons of torpedo plant workers waited for the man in white every Saturday afternoon.

Snacks

The po'boy sandwich was created during the depression (or just before it). Some historians claim Clovis and Benny Martin assembled the first one in 1927. All agree New Orleans is birthplace to the French or Italian loaf that is halved horizontally and filled with sliced meat, tomatoes and lettuce. Another New Orleans sandwich, the peacemaker, holds hot poached oysters and is said to have been carried home by husbands after a late night out.

Sandwiches similar to po'boys appeared with names like hero, grinder, hoagie or submarine—so-called by the men at the New London submarine base where they were exceedingly popular. Also a 1930s creation was the Reuben, named for Reuben's Delicatessen in New York, with two slices of rye bread, corned beef, sauerkraut, Swiss cheese and Russian dressing.

As accompaniments to sandwiches, grocery stores began to carry ready-made potato chips after 1929 when Freeman McBeth of the J. D. Ferry Company developed the first continuous chip cooker and installed it at the Ross Potato Chip Company in Richland, Pennsylvania. In 1933, Dixie Wax Paper Company of Dallas perfected the preprinted, waxed glassine bag for chips and other snacks like popcorn, peanuts and pretzels.

Pretzels had been made commercially in America since before the Civil War, but in 1933 the Reading Pretzel Machinery Company brought out the first automatic twisting machine. About the same time, I. J. Filler of San Antonio was granted a trademark for "Corn Chips," evolved from tortillas, and—independently—Elmer Doolin paid $100 for the recipe for "Fritos" and a hand-operated corn-chip maker from a Mexican eager to leave San Antonio and go back home.

A favorite dessert in 1930 was the Twinkie, created to bolster cake sales that gloomy year by James A. Dewar of Continental Baking. The cream-freighted sponge cake got its name from a billboard Dewar saw advertising Twinkle Toe Shoes. Its original banana-puree filling was a casualty of World War II, when bananas were scarce and plain vanilla filling had to be substituted.

Brownies

1/2 cup butter	1 teaspoon vanilla extract
4 squares unsweetened	1 cup sifted flour
chocolate	1 cup coarsely chopped
2 cups sugar	pecans or walnuts (optional)
2 eggs	

Melt butter with chocolate in a heavy pan over low heat. Remove from the stove and stir in sugar. Beat in eggs, one at a time, and add vanilla extract. Stir in flour and, if you like, chopped pecans or walnuts. Spoon the mixture into a buttered 8-by-10-inch pan and bake at 325°F for 30 to 35 minutes. Cool the brownies before cutting squares and serving them.

Ginger Shortbread

1-1/2 cups flour	1/2 teaspoon salt
1/2 cup superfine sugar	8 tablespoons
1 teaspoon ginger	softened butter

Sift flour, sugar, ginger and salt into a bowl. Rub butter into the flour mixture. Gather the dough into a ball, place it on a buttered baking sheet and pat it into a flat disk about 1/2 inch thick. Indent the edge with the tines of a fork, prick the middle repeatedly and score the disk into 8 wedges. Bake in a 350°F oven for 20 minutes or until golden. Divide it into wedges along the scored lines but let it cool on the sheet for at least 15 minutes.

Streamlined Kitchens

The depression spurred inventors, although most families could not afford to buy the new creations. In fact, only about 60 percent of city homes and 10 percent of farms had electricity in 1930. By 1940, more than 90 percent of city-dwellers, but less than 40 percent of farmers, had it.

Nonetheless, nearly half of all American homes boasted an electric or gas refrigerator by 1940. The earliest common refrigerant had been sulphur dioxide, which was toxic. In 1931, a Frigidaire team, headed by Thomas Midgely, Jr., determined chlorofluorocarbons were both safe and effective. (Their effect on the Earth's ozone layer was not anticipated.) Dupont's version, trademarked Freon

12, was accepted industry-wide. The new refrigerant was sealed inside a box coated with pastel-colored porcelain enamel to match the new tinted kitchen stoves. This refrigerator kept foods fresh longer than an icebox had, ending a need for daily shopping and letting shoppers take advantage of supermarket sales.

During the 1930s, the kitchen sink was designed to slip into the top of a cabinet rather than stand on its own legs. At the end of the decade, the stove was streamlined and squared off to merge with cabinets. One or two ovens went under the burners, and any excess space beneath them was used for storage drawers.

Wonder brand bread came out with presliced loaves in 1930, a novelty that was soon embraced as a time saver. Both white and wheat Wonder Bread was stocked in this Wisconsin food store. FSA photo by John Vachon, Greendale, Wisconsin, 1939.

The Waring Blendor named for the famous dance-band leader Fred Waring of the 1930s was marketed to home cooks then. It was patented in 1922 by Stephen J. Poplawski of Racine, Wisconsin, the home of Horlick Corporation, makers of malted milk powder. It was sold only to drugstores before Waring invested in it in 1936 and hired marketers to popularize it as a home blender. (Waring thought the final o in the spelling set the gadget apart from competitors. The name was Waring's chief contribution.)

Vita-Mania

Although scientists recognized the existence of vitamins and minerals in food, they did not know how much of these elements were necessary in human diet. Claims that now sound ridiculous were made by college professors as well as charlatans: Vitamin B was "brain food." Vitamin C prevented tooth decay.

Advertisers rushed to claim health-giving properties for their foods and banish worries that milling and canning robbed foods of their nutrients. In 1930, the Department

Salmon Loaf

Similar loaves substitute cooked rice or mashed potatoes for bread cubes. Some add chopped green or ripe olives, or a tablespoon or two of chopped fresh dill.

3 cups flaked, cooked salmon
3 cups fresh bread cubes
3 eggs
3/4 cup milk
2 tablespoons melted butter
1/4 cup chopped parsley
2 tablespoons chopped onion
juice of 1 lemon
salt and pepper
tomato sauce or hollandaise sauce

Combine salmon with bread cubes. Stir in eggs lightly beaten with milk and melted butter. Add parsley, onion, the lemon juice and salt and pepper. Spoon the mixture into a buttered 8-cup loaf pan. Bake at 375°F for 45 minutes. Serve from the pan or unmolded. Accompany with tomato sauce or hollandaise. Serves 6.

Even during the lean years of the 1930s, a fair meant homemade baked goods, cakes and pies. This event was held, appropriately enough, in Pie Town, New Mexico. Photo by Russell Lee.

of Agriculture praised both white and whole wheat bread as "economical sources of energy and protein." Yet when techniques for synthesizing vitamins were discovered in 1935, drugstores and grocers rushed to get supplies of vitamin pills and liquids. And consumers hurried to buy them.

Pure Foods

The 1906 Pure Food and Drug Act was amended routinely over the years. Sometimes changes were made to suit scientists who disagreed with Dr. Wiley; more often they were meant to please politicians whose constituents included food interests. By the 1930s, the Act was in shambles.

Roosevelt's Assistant Secretary of Agriculture, Rexford Guy Tugwell, campaigned aggressively for a new law. Public opinion seemed to support him. In 1933 *100,000,000 Guinea Pigs* by Arthur Kallet and F. J. Schlink roused national anger in much the same way that Sinclair's *The Jungle* had done. Tugwell wanted foods rated

Dirty Rice

The name of this dish is a joking reference to its appearance; the bits of chicken give the rice a brown or "dirty" look.

1/2 pound chicken gizzards	1 green pepper
1/2 pound chicken livers	1 celery rib
2 onions	1 cup white rice
1 tablespoon oil	salt and pepper
2 tablespoons minced parsley	

Wash and trim chicken gizzards and livers; mince them together with onions, green pepper and celery rib. Stirring occasionally, cook mixture in 1 tablespoon oil for about 1 hour. Meanwhile, steam or boil 1 cup white rice. When the chicken mixture is a rich brown, toss it with the cooked rice. Season with salt and pepper. Stir in 2 tablespoons minced parsley. Serves 4 to 6.

Liver and Onions

1 large onion	4 thin slices calf's liver
4 tablespoons butter	flour seasoned with salt
1 tablespoon oil	and pepper

Cut onion into thin slices and sauté in 2 tablespoons butter in a heavy skillet until soft and golden. Meanwhile, melt remaining 2 tablespoons butter in oil over medium heat in another skillet. Dust liver slices with seasoned flour and sauté them for about 1 minute on each side. Transfer the liver to a heated platter and spoon the onion over them. Serves 2.

for quality; he asked for more accurate labeling and he insisted ingredients be itemized. However, food manufacturers lobbied so fiercely that the final bill was not passed until 1938, at which point it was nearly as full of loopholes as Wiley's had been.

Wine and Spirits

Prohibition took two years to enact—and eight months to repeal. The Twenty-First Amendment was proposed by Congress on February 20, 1933, and took effect December 5, although some states and counties within states chose to remain "dry" for many decades more.

Cocktail parties grew increasingly popular when the drinks could be made from palatable and safe whiskey. The repertory of mixed drinks burgeoned as spirits were mixed with one another and flavorings that ranged from cucumber strips to maraschino cherries. The names were as exotic as the drinks: pink lady, morning glory, angel's dream. Hostesses found that cocktail parties staged as open houses lasting for several hours (typically 5 p.m. to 7 p.m.) proved a wonderful way to entertain lots of friends at one event.

In this 1933 print by Howard Cook entitled *Taxco Market,* Mexican vendors display their goods on blankets spread on the ground, most likely offering items such as tortillas, tamales and hot peppers.

Visiting an aircraft factory in 1943, Eleanor Roosevelt is served a "victory lunch," the same meal the factory workers eat. This highly nutritious lunch, which cost 47 cents in the plant cafeteria, consisted of a small steak, two vegetables, a salad, enriched bread, custard and a glass of milk.

Chapter Seven
Blackouts and Mr. Black (1940–1945)

*D*espite shortages and rations, most Americans ate better than ever during World War II. The Lend-Lease program, begun in 1941 to supply Britain with arms, propelled the nation into affluence.

With America's entry into the war after Pearl Harbor was bombed on December 7, 1941, the nation geared up to produce military materiel. New factories across the country made universal employment possible. Faced with the need to feed its allies as well as its own military and civilians, the nation subsidized farmers so that they could buy more livestock and fertilizer. As a result, agricultural production rose about 250 percent even though farmhands by the thousands had volunteered for service, were drafted or moved to higher-paying factory jobs.

Increasing farm supplies, of course, did not compensate for imports lost as shipping was diverted to military needs. Nor did the food stretch far enough to meet every demand. As America met the same shortages that had marked 1918, it tried to solve them the same way: meatless Tuesdays and Fridays, home gardens, reduced portions, substitutions.

Nonetheless, families that had been on relief for a decade now had at least one wage earner, and they could indulge occasionally in steaks and lobsters. Servicemen and women were allowed almost twice as much food as civilians—in theory, 5 1/4 pounds daily compared to 3. Although they complained about the "chow," the military consumed 60 percent of prime and choice meats and 80 percent of utility grade. They had fresh-baked bread three times a day and lots of ice cream whenever the Quartermaster Corps could manage it.

Fried Tomatoes

6 bacon slices, cut into 1-inch pieces	flour
6 green or firm red tomatoes	1/2 cup brown sugar
	1 cup cream

Fry the bacon in a large skillet. Drain the bacon and pour off all but a few spoonfuls of its fat. Slice tomatoes about 1/2 inch thick; dust both sides with flour. Fry the tomato slices until they brown on one side. Sprinkle the slices with brown sugar, turn them and brown the other side. Add cream and simmer the slices for 5 minutes. Transfer tomatoes and sauce to a platter and sprinkle them with the bacon bits. Serves 6.

Everybody's War

In 1940, the population was a tad above 132 million; more than twelve million went into the armed forces during the first year of the war. By V-J Day on August 15, 1945, sixteen million American men and women (more than 10 percent of the population) had served stateside or in the European or Pacific theaters.

To add to family dislocation, approximately three million wives followed their husbands to

OURS...to fight for

FREEDOM FROM WANT

This poster by Norman Rockwell reminded Americans that one of the freedoms they were fighting for in World War II was the "freedom from want," appropriately symbolized by a Thanksgiving dinner.

Split Pea Soup

1 cup dried split peas	1 carrot, chopped
water	2 celery ribs, chopped
2-inch cube of salt pork	1 bay leaf
or a turkey carcass	1/2 teaspoon thyme
1 onion, chopped	

Soak split peas in water for several hours. Drain them, and add enough fresh water to make 2 quarts. Combine the peas and water in a heavy pan, add salt pork or turkey carcass, chopped onion, carrot, celery ribs, bay leaf and thyme. Bring to a boil, cover, then simmer for 2 hours. Stir occasionally and add more water if needed. Discard the pork or carcass. Puree the soup with a food mill or sieve. Season to taste. Serves 6.

army or navy bases. An additional twenty-three million civilians changed addresses in search of jobs. Close to one and a half million of these wound up in California; a similar number of southerners migrated north. Regional food patterns shifted as grits and chili reached Detroit while Dallas met sauerkraut and wurst.

Slowly at the beginning, and then in a deluge, women filled factory and office jobs left vacant by draftees. In total, six million women—many of them mothers of small children—worked full-time or part-time.

Rationing on the Home Front

In April 1941, the government established the OPA—Office of Price Administration—to prevent spiraling prices, profiteering and inflation. Production of many civilian goods ceased or diminished. Metal, rubber, leather, fabric (including silk and nylon), fur, even paper were needed by the military. Trains, trucks, ships and airplanes had to carry servicemen and arms. For civilians, the motto was "Use it up, wear it out, make it do, or do without."

As men went to war, women took up factory jobs to help supply the nation and fuel the war machine. Here women workers eat lunch in a factory in Iowa. Photo by Jack Delano, 1943.

Accordingly, in April 1942, the OPA froze prices on about six thousand foods. Sugar was rationed when Philippine imports ended. Ships that might have carried sugar from Cuba or Puerto Rico were needed elsewhere. (After Caribbean shipping reopened, increased military need kept sugar rationed until 1946.)

Americans who remembered World War I shortages stocked up on 100-pound bags of sugar early in 1942. When signing for ration books, however, everyone was asked to declare how much sugar they had on hand. Some lied with nonchalance, but most hoarders confessed and lost stamps representing whatever amount they admitted to owning. The ration of 8 (later 12) ounces per family member per week sounds generous; but many women baked cakes and pies daily and put up their own fruit and jelly, so sugar went fast.

In November 1942, coffee was rationed, again due to lack of space on ships. In February 1943, canned goods were rationed because of metal shortages and the need to send food overseas in cans. During March 1943, butter, cheese, fish and meats were in short supply and rationed.

By then, the housewife—and grocer and food wholesaler and processor—were dealing with hundreds of flimsy little blue and red stamps, representing 1, 2, 5 or 8 points. Everyone in a family had a separate ration book and was entitled to 48 blue points (canned fruit and vegetables) and 64 red points (meat, fish, butter, cheese) per month. Stamps also were needed for sugar and coffee and for the shoes and gas to go to the grocer.

Necessary though it was, rationing proved a colossal nuisance. A housewife shopping for a family of four could spend 192 blue points per month and 256 red points. Stamps were valid for about thirty days—often starting and ending mid-month. Stamps for canned foods might be valid from March 22 to April 25, while those for meat were usable from March 1 to March 31; all were worthless before or after those dates.

A cook needed to plan menus ahead and budget stamps as carefully as money. Points were assigned to products on the basis of desirability and ever changing availability. Thus, sirloin steak always required more points than hamburger did, but values on both could shift overnight. A poor harvest sent up the value of

Peach Brown Betty

1 cup graham cracker crumbs	4 large ripe peaches
1/4 cup melted butter or margarine	1 tablespoon lemon juice
	1/4 cup cider or water
1 cup brown sugar	heavy cream (optional)
1 teaspoon grated lemon peel	lemon sauce (optional)
1/4 teaspoon nutmeg	1 teaspoon cinnamon

Mix graham cracker crumbs with melted butter or margarine and set aside. Combine brown sugar, lemon peel, cinnamon and nutmeg; set aside. Peel, halve, pit and slice peaches. Arrange half of the peach slices in a buttered 8-cup baking dish. Sprinkle with 1 tablespoon lemon juice, one-half of the sugar mixture and one-third of the crumbs. Repeat the layers, ending with crumbs. Drizzle cider or water over the top. Bake at 375°F for 30 minutes until the peaches are tender and the top brown. Serve hot with heavy cream or a lemon sauce made by cooking 1/2 cup sugar and 1 tablespoon cornstarch in 1 cup water over low heat until thick, then stirring in 2 tablespoons butter and 2 tablespoons lemon juice. Serves 4 to 6.

Fried Cornmeal Mush

Colonists actually called cornmeal mush hasty pudding because it cooked fast by their standards.

1 cup cornmeal
4 cups lightly salted boiling water
bacon drippings, butter or margarine
maple syrup, honey or jam

Stirring constantly, gradually pour cornmeal into boiling water. Reduce the heat to very low, cover and simmer for 60 minutes; stir occasionally. Pour this mush into a loaf pan and refrigerate overnight or until firm. Unmold and cut the mush into 1/2-inch slices. Fry the slices in bacon drippings, butter or margarine until browned on both sides. Serve with maple syrup, honey or jam. Serves 6.

canned fruit. A cheese surplus meant the points would drop, although the price might not. (So much butterfat went into cheese that butter was often hard to find.) Poultry was not rationed, nor were meals at restaurants or company cafeterias.

Even when a shopper had enough valid stamps, the supplier might not have scarce meats and canned goods. A queue formed when word went out that a grocer had a supply of coffee or a butcher had steaks in his locker. Candy, even the penny variety, became scarce. Ice cream makers had to stick to eight flavors. Wheat was in such demand that millers experimented with soy flour as an extender (and unexpected source of protein) in all-purpose and pancake flours.

Thirsty Americans downed nearly 190 million gallons of whiskey in 1942 compared to 140 million gallons in 1940. Stocks of imported spirits were exhausted quickly, and domestic whiskey nearly disappeared as distillers turned to the industrial alcohol needed for explosives. Brewers ran low on beer and had no cans. French and German wines were replaced by domestic varieties. Moonshiners opened their stills again, and exotic kinds of rum and gin arrived from Latin America.

Snowballs

1 cup butter or margarine	1 cup milk
1 cup sugar	1 teaspoon vanilla
4 eggs, separated	white frosting
2 cups flour	grated coconut (optional)
2 teaspoons baking powder	

Cream butter or margarine with sugar until light and fluffy. Beat in egg yolks, one at a time. Sift flour with baking powder and add to the batter alternately with milk. Stir in vanilla. Beat egg whites until stiff but not dry and fold them in gently. Spoon batter into buttered muffin pans and bake at 375°F for 25 minutes or until a toothpick inserted into a cupcake comes out clean. Cool on wire racks, then spread white icing over the tops and sides of the cakes. If desired, sprinkle them with grated coconut. Makes about 24.

Beating the System

Most Americans accepted rationing as calmly as they did the nightly "blackouts" when shades were drawn to darken possible targets from enemy air attack. Others treated rationing as a sporting challenge. They cajoled or bribed butchers and grocers into setting aside the rare cuts of meat or the fancy canned goods. Grocers, eager to unload slow-selling stock, promoted "tie-ins" allowing a cook to buy desirable merchandise only by purchasing the white elephants.

Some shoppers, particularly those in large cities where skepticism prevailed, circumvented the rules by patronizing "Mr. Black." Like the bootlegger of the 1920s, the black marketer could supply anything for a price: sugar, meat, canned fruit, even ration stamps. Cattle rustling became a problem in western states; social historian Richard Lingeman reports that more than 10 percent of civilian meat was farm-slaughtered and sold without benefit of ration coupons.

Horsemeat debuted in St. Louis when meat rationing did; butchers across the nation did a lively business in this slightly sweet meat. Montana tried to promote buffalo to red-meat lovers, but failed to find converts. Domestic rabbit grew in popularity, and hunters supplied game animals.

A convenient way to get one-up on meat rationing was to save cooking fats for redemption at the butcher shop. The cook could expect 4 cents and 2 ration points for each pound turned in. (A pound of fat would yield the glycerin needed to manufacture a pound of gunpowder—enough for fifty 30-caliber bullets.)

Victory Gardens

The liberty gardens of World War I inspired the government to encourage citizens to plant victory gardens wherever there was vacant land (or a plowable lawn or flower bed). A scholarly contributor to the *Los Angeles Times* pointed out that the term "victory garden" dated to a 1603 book with that name by Richard Gardner. "If any citie or towne should be besieged with the enemy, what better provision for the greatest number of people can be than every garden to be sufficiently planted with carrots?"

Although never under siege, Americans planted vegetables in backyards, in the zoo at Portland, Oregon, and in Chicago's Arlington Race Track. Many gardens were no more than a few square feet; others encompassed acres. In 1943, some twenty million gardens yielded about one million tons of vegetables worth at least $85 million.

The gardens introduced many Americans to the pleasures of eating fresh produce. And the inevitable shortages of seeds for common vegetables led thousands to experiment with oddities like Swiss chard and brussels sprouts, and later incorporate these permanently into their diets. Home canning soared with about three-quarters of American families putting up an average of 165 jars a year. Toward the end of the war, enthusiasm for gardening waned, but harvest shows—in movie theater lobbies as well as at county fairs—kept children and adults, alike, at work.

Stuffed Green Peppers

4 large green peppers	1 tablespoon chopped parsley
1/2 pound ground beef	1/2 teaspoon paprika
1 small onion, chopped	salt and pepper
1 cup boiled rice	1 cup water
1/2 cup drained	tomato sauce
canned tomato	

Cut the tops off the peppers, remove the seeds and membranes, then parboil the peppers and their tops for 10 minutes. Drain these cases and lids upside down. Meanwhile, sauté ground beef and onion until no trace of pink shows in the beef, and the onion is soft. Off the heat, add boiled rice, drained canned tomato, parsley, paprika plus salt and pepper to taste. Stand the peppers in a deep baking dish. Pack the beef mixture into them and cover the cases with their lids. Pour about 1 cup of water into the dish around the peppers. Bake at 350°F for 30 minutes, adding water to the dish if needed. Serve the peppers with tomato sauce.

Innovations

Recipes stressed the patriotism a cook showed by saving food. Betty Crocker counseled that "American homemakers are called upon to help preserve democracy and save the peace by saving food so the hungry may eat." Among her ideas was extending hamburger with Wheaties and enriching scalloped potatoes with bologna.

Honey, molasses, corn syrup and saccharin took the place of sugar as a sweetener. None worked just right in conventional recipes, so home economists developed special formulas for desserts made with one or another. Even so, housewives baked less and put up fewer jams and marmalades.

Margarine, long considered "poor man's butter," got new respect. By the 1920s, manufacturers were making it from vegetable oil, hydrogenated so that it was solid at room temperature. Its texture and taste were close to those of butter; it looked buttery after being mixed with the capsule of food dye enclosed in its package. And while butter required precious red coupons, margarine did not; sales nearly doubled from 1941 to 1945.

With food rationing once again limiting the availability of meat, it was necessary to stretch it as far as possible. Here a Wartime Food Demonstrator explains methods of "extending" beef by adding cereal to a meatloaf. A sprig of parsley adds the finishing touch. FSA photo by Ann Rosener, Washington, D.C., 1943.

Families who rejected margarine attempted to stretch butter by whipping it with gelatin and milk or light cream. Coffee drinkers who extended coffee by adding chicory found the combination bitter, but were probably happier than those who tried to use coffee grounds twice. Ersatz products such as the cereal-based Postum gained new customers, at least until coffee rationing ended in July 1943.

Icebox Cookies

This recipe can be varied by adding 1/2 cup chopped nuts or candied fruit, 1/4 cup cocoa or 1 melted square unsweetened chocolate, or by substituting almond extract or a few drops of peppermint oil for the vanilla extract.

1/2 cup butter or margarine	1 teaspoon vanilla
1 cup sugar	1-1/2 cups flour
1 egg	1 teaspoon baking powder

Cream butter or margarine with sugar. Stir in egg, vanilla extract, and flour sifted with baking powder. Shape the dough into a 2-inch cylinder, wrap it in waxed paper and chill overnight or until very firm. Cut off 1/4-inch slices and bake on ungreased baking sheets at 350°F for about 8 minutes until lightly browned. Makes 4 or 5 dozen.

Wartime Cookery

Young wives following their husbands from base to base often found housing substandard and resorted to cooking on a hot plate. Women who worked at defense plants could spare little time to fix traditional food for their families. One-dish meals, whether stews or casseroles, were popular. Vegetables, particularly those from the back yard, got special attention. Entrées based on cheese or eggs rose in favor—Welsh rabbit, soufflé, macaroni and cheese and such.

To help the busy housewife, Gold Medal flour introduced the "one-bowl cake." All dry ingredients were sifted into a bowl, then shortening and liquid added. The cake was not as tender as one made conventionally, but families enjoyed its freshness (as later they appreciated cake-mix cakes).

Military Rations

American servicemen came first, no matter what other allocation of food there might be. Depending on how far they were from the front, they ate A, B, C, or K rations. In stateside mess halls, they got A rations, or perishable foods; meals may not have tasted like mother's, yet most servicemen gained weight during basic training. B rations came from a mess hall overseas; most foods were canned or packaged. These kitchens made Spam famous and immortalized creamed chipped beef (disparagingly called "S.O.S." or "shit on a shingle").

C and K rations were designed for eating away from camp, perhaps at the front. In the original C ration, six cans furnished three meals. Besides the obvious disadvantage of being heavy to tote around, cans had to be buried when emptied. Otherwise, as some troops found, the enemy could follow their movements by the glitter of discarded metal. K rations designed by nutritionist Ansel Keyes lightened the load by combining canned and dried foods. (Sadly, not until 1944 did the army include halazone tablets to purify water, without which much of the dried food was worthless.) Both C and K rations were supplemented with D rations: "chocolate bars" of cocoa fat, sucrose, oat flour and skim milk that tasted even worse than that mix sounds.

The Basic Seven

The government was shocked when some 40 percent of the first million men drafted for military service were rejected on medical grounds, often for conditions such as tooth decay or bad vision that were attributable to poor diet.

To "make America strong by making Americans stronger," the National Research Council's Committee on Food and Nutrition set about determining scientific dietary standards

Red Beans and Rice

Servicemen sampled foods from many parts of the country as they were transferred from one training camp to another during the war. Northerners learned to like this Creole favorite, in which the beans were often cooked with pickled or salt pork and dressed with tomatoes and chopped garlic stewed in bacon fat.

> 2 cups (1 pound) red kidney or pinto beans
> 1/2 cup chopped scallions, plus some for garnish
> 1/2 cup chopped onions
> 2 tablespoons bacon fat or lard
> 1 quart water
> 1 leftover ham bone or 2 meaty smoked ham hocks
> freshly cooked white rice

Soak kidney or pinto beans in water overnight. In a large pot, sauté chopped scallions and onions in bacon fat or lard. Drain beans and add them to the pot with 1 quart water and ham bone or ham hocks. Bring to a boil, reduce the heat, cover and simmer very slowly for about 2 hours or until the beans are tender. Remove the ham, cut the meat off the bones and dice it; discard the bones and add the meat to the beans. Mash the softest beans against the sides of the pot to make a sauce for the remaining beans. Taste and season with salt and pepper. Serve freshly cooked white rice and chopped scallions with the beans. Serves 6.

Creamed Chipped Beef

This is a glorified version of the "S.O.S." served in army mess halls.

> 1/4 cup chopped onion
> 1/4 cup chopped green pepper
> 4 tablespoons drippings, butter or margarine
> 3 tablespoons flour
> 2 cups milk
> 1 teaspoon dry mustard
> cayenne pepper
> 1/2 pound dried chipped beef
> hot toast

Sauté chopped onion and green pepper in drippings, butter or margarine until soft. Mix in flour. Stir in milk. When this mixture thickens, reduce the heat. Season with dry mustard and a few grains of cayenne pepper. Stir in dried chipped beef cut into thin shreds; heat it through. If needed, thin the sauce with additional milk. Serve on hot toast. Serves 4.

During an inspection tour in Tunisia in 1943, General Dwight D. Eisenhower stops for a noon mess of C rations, the portable, canned meals eaten by the troops.

once and for all, calling on physicians, home economists and chemists for advice. The result was the 1941 table of Recommended Daily Allowances for the number of calories as well as the amount of protein and eight other nutrients that people of different ages and conditions should consume.

Experts classified foods in 1943 into seven groups, each of which supplied essential dietary elements. Posters and lectures spread the word about the "basic seven": milk, lean meat or fish, potatoes or apples, eggs, bread or cereal, green or yellow vegetables, oranges or tomatoes. Fats and sweets were excluded, or introduced "as you like them."

In late 1942, the government decreed that flour for the military should be enriched with thiamin and other vitamins. By 1943, just about all commercially baked bread was made with this enriched flour. Advertisers got on the nutrition bandwagon, promoting whole-grain or

Chicken Soufflé with Mushrooms

An easy but elegant main dish that could be cooked quickly.

>   1 cup diced cooked chicken
>   1 8-ounce can mushrooms, drained and diced
>   1 can condensed cream of chicken soup
>   6 eggs, separated

Combine chicken, mushrooms and cream of chicken soup in a large saucepan. Season to taste. Heat through. Off the stove, stir in 6 well-beaten egg yolks. Let the mixture cool for 5 minutes. Meanwhile, beat 6 egg whites until they form stiff peaks. Fold egg whites into chicken mixture. Pour into ungreased 8-cup soufflé dish or casserole. Bake at 400°F for 25 minutes or until the soufflé is puffed and golden brown. Serves 6.

"restored" cereals and breads, healthful citrus fruit, even vitamin-rich catsup. Candy makers stressed the quick energy their products were said to supply and noted it was included in field rations.

Gourmet Magazine

Against all odds—food rations, paper shortages, lack of personnel—Earle R. MacAusland started *Gourmet* in 1941. Written to appeal to men as well as women, the magazine espoused cooking from scratch with fresh vegetables and fruits in season. As MacAusland wrote in the first issue, "Good food and good living have always been a great American tradition. At our fingertips lie an abundance and variety of foods unequaled anywhere."

Although directed primarily at an upper-class audience, the magazine contended that anyone who shopped and cooked carefully could enjoy fine food and wine whatever their budget. Paradoxically, the middle-class *American Cookery*—descended from *The Boston Cooking School Magazine*—stopped publication in the 1940s as the aristocratic *Gourmet* thrived.

Chapter Eight
The Boom Times (1945–1960)

*W*hat celebrations were held when World War II ended in August 1945! Parades and dancing in the streets welcomed soldiers and sailors home. Prosperity proved to be one of the war's chief legacies. There were jobs enough at last. The college education most Americans never expected was attainable with the GI Bill of Rights, which also guaranteed veterans low-interest mortgages. Nearly 1.5 million homes were built by 1950, usually at the edge of town where land was cheap. Thus, suburbia was built—and, for ambitious commuters, exurbia.

Most married women, although quick to accept jobs in wartime, now left them. Average family income rose from $1,231 in 1939 to $2,854 in 1947. The typical husband earned enough so that his wife could stay home to raise their children—thirty million of them born from 1942 to 1950, with the baby boom lasting until 1960.

Nothing Like Mom Used to Make

The depression and war had conspired to wipe away memories of day-to-day indulgence in elegant food. Young wives with growing families and no servants prided themselves on ingenuity and took advantage of every cooking short-cut they found. A handful of gourmets might look down their noses at breakfast from a box and dinner from cans, but for many cooks "quick and easy" or "heat and serve" were magic phrases.

Condensed soups became indispensable ingredients for the casseroles that remained popular because they were easy to put together. Pasta and rice were favorite bases for these assemblages. In one unforgettable tuna casserole, macaroni provided smoothness and potato chips gave crunch.

Americans could afford to indulge in beef—hamburgers if the budget was tight, 2-inch Porterhouse steaks on payday. Consumption of beef rose from 55 pounds per person in

---

Sloppy Joes

The name appeared around 1960, but sloppy joes were familiar to teenagers long before that.

>   2 pounds ground beef
>   1 tablespoon oil
>   1 cup finely chopped onion
>   1/2 cup finely chopped green pepper
>   1 cup water
>   1/2 cup catsup or chili sauce
>   2 tablespoons Worcestershire sauce
>   salt and pepper
>   8 toasted hamburger buns

Brown ground beef in oil, breaking the beef up well. Add chopped onion and green pepper; stir for 4 or 5 minutes or until the onion is soft. Mix in water, catsup or chili sauce, Worcestershire sauce and salt and pepper to taste. Cover and simmer for about 10 minutes. Spoon onto toasted hamburger buns. Serve hot.

At the end of World War II, the catchwords for cooks were convenience and economy. This 1956 *Look* magazine advertisement for Libby's canned foods has the company's home economist telling women to "think of all the easy-do meals you can fix!"

1940 to 85 pounds in 1960. Sales of pork, veal and lamb fell, but annual chicken consumption doubled from 14 pounds per person in 1940 to 28 in 1960, as the price stayed seductively low.

Poultry growers had known since ancient times that some breeds of chicken laid more eggs, some produced better meat. Research work led to hybrid hens that laid three hundred eggs annually for 2 years or more, and to other meatier hybrids ready for sale as broilers or fryers at 2 months or as roasters at 4 months. In the 1950s, producers increased the size of coops to house thousands of birds; research into lighting, food and medicine helped to ensure healthy flocks.

Feasting Outdoors

Charcoal smoke endowed beefsteaks with ineffable flavor, and the briquettes widely available after the war were easy to light. Acceptance of the backyard barbecue spread swiftly north from the Sun Belt to make cooking a family affair: Dad oversaw the main course on the grill while Mom brought accompaniments from the kitchen.

Handymen dug up their backyards to lay flagstone or brick patios and construct huge masonry monuments to the barbecue. Home magazines published plans for barbecues that included space for baking as well as grilling. Those who didn't want such edifices used portable grills, the least demanding but most expensive of which were gas-fired. (Liquid smoke from a bottle was said to impart charcoal flavor.)

How to make a
SOUPER CASSEROLE

Campbell's soups became a staple ingredient in casseroles, one-dish meals that could be made in a jiffy. This Souper Tuna Casserole calls for whole potato chips as a topping as well as one cup of crushed potato chips as an ingredient in the casserole. Ad from *Good Housekeeping* magazine, November 1956.

Here's the souper answer to a nourishing one-dish dinner — a last-minute meal — a company-coming supper! It's a Souper Casserole, the time-saving, budget-saving recipe for a meal to please everyone. And the secret is soup. Take any Campbell's Cream Soup, for soup adds the just-right seasoning, that extra bounce of flavor and appetizing smoothness. You can have this supper ready in 25 minutes.

SOUPER TUNA CASSEROLE

1 can Cream of Mushroom Soup
½ cup milk
1 cup drained, cooked peas
7-oz. can drained, flaked tuna
1 cup crushed potato chips
Whole potato chips

In a 1-quart casserole, combine soup, milk, peas, tuna and crushed potato chips. Top with potato chips, garnish with pimiento. Then slip your casserole into a moderate oven (375°F) for 25 minutes. 4 servings.

Campbell's
CONDENSED
CREAM OF
MUSHROOM
SOUP

Good cooks cook with *Campbell's Soups*

Entertainment

Barbecuing fostered casual entertaining. Patio parties held across adjoining yards were regular weekend affairs. Even when families were busy or broke, they could manage potluck or covered-dish suppers.

Progressive parties were stylish; each course was served at a different home to minimize cooking for all of the hostesses. Travel could be a logistical nightmare, however, with guests arriving early, getting lost or dropping out. Theme parties rated high, too, because they provided an almost ready-made scheme for decorating the table and a chance to experiment with strange foods.

Even when entertaining her husband's boss and his wife, a middle-class American wife felt comfortable serving a menu of processed foods: canned shrimp with bottled sauce, canned ham decorated with canned pineapple, canned green beans and a cake-mix dessert. A favorite salad was a glob of cottage cheese centered in the hollow of a canned peach half and garnished by a bottled green maraschino cherry, all plopped astride a leaf of iceberg lettuce. (As a measure of the salad's ubiquity, annual cottage cheese consumption jumped from 2 pounds per person in 1940 to 5 pounds in 1960.)

High Spirits

In suburbia, where everybody was a newcomer, liquor was the quicker way to relax guests and socialize. Cocktail parties ranged from catered

The backyard barbecue became a popular style of cooking and entertaining. The husband generally took care of grilling the meat, while the wife prepared side dishes and salad. This photo was taken by a photographer from the *New York World-Telegram and Sun*.

Steak Barbecued in a Salt Casing

President Dwight D. Eisenhower enjoyed barbecuing meat—according to the press releases—and this was said to be his favorite recipe.

> prepared mustard
> sirloin, porterhouse, T-bone or
> tenderloin steak, cut 2 inches thick
> coarse salt

Spread prepared mustard on both sides of steak. Moisten coarse salt with water and pack a 1/2-inch layer of salt onto one side of the steak, pressing it in well. Cover with a paper towel to hold the salt, then turn the steak over and repeat on the other side. Place the steak in a basket grill, then barbecue 4 to 6 inches from ash-covered coals for about 12 minutes on each side to get rare beef, 15 minutes for medium steak and 18 minutes for well done. The paper will burn off during cooking. When the beef is done, take it out of the basket, break off the salt and serve on a hot platter.

Liptauer Cheese

Cheese balls were one way cooks could use foods like anchovies and capers.

3 ounces softened cream cheese
6 tablespoons butter
1 tablespoon finely minced chives
1 teaspoon capers
2 anchovy fillets
1/2 teaspoon caraway seeds

Mash softened cream cheese with butter. Add chives, capers, anchovy fillets and caraway seeds. Beat until smooth. Shape into a ball or press into a small mold, wrap in aluminum foil, refrigerate for at least 3 hours to let the flavors blend. Serve with pumpernickel bread or wheat crackers.

triumphs, with hired bartenders and waiters, to BYOB (bring your own bottle) affairs. Whatever the style, a neighborhood often developed a cocktail circuit with a regular sequence of hosts and predictable guests.

The popular mixed drinks were old-fashioneds, Manhattans and martinis. For adventure, drinkers experimented with tequila and sake and a cabinet's worth of liqueurs. Sweet mixes associated with wartime whiskey, colas or ginger ale, lost out to tangier tonic water and soda water in highballs (a term that had begun to sound old-hat even then). Tomato and orange juice were *de rigueur* for stylish bloody Marys and screwdrivers; fresh lemon juice was essential for daiquiris and bottled lime juice for gimlets.

During the 1950s, sales of gin rose from six to nineteen million gallons. Vodka was rare at the start of that decade, but in 1960 Americans downed nine million gallons of it—presumably believing the old wives' tale that nobody could smell vodka on a drinker's breath.

Party-givers created fancy tidbits; the laziest might enliven canned liver paste with drops of brandy. A landmark was Lipton's 1954 introduction of dried onion soup mix with a label carrying the recipe for California dip (whisk contents with sour cream). Raw vegetables and potato chips were familiar, but dips were new—and admirably simple.

Westinghouse took cooking outdoors one step further with the portable patio cart, an appliance that could be rolled outside and plugged in with an extension cord. In this 1960 photo, a breakfast of eggs, ham and toast is ready for serving.

Because Prohibition and the Great Depression wreaked havoc in American vineyards, fine wine was imported, expensive and rare as an aperitif or accompaniment to food. A few vintners began putting modestly priced wine into gallon containers, and this "jug wine" found a market among adventurous diners as well as immigrants who preserved old-world customs and servicemen who had developed a taste for wine overseas.

Ready in an Instant

In wartime, processors learned a lot about preserving food. Now Quartermaster Corps technology came home. French's dried instant potatoes introduced in 1946, for example, scored a hit with American families. A child could make mashed potatoes with it, and many did.

In 1947 and 1948, General Mills and Pillsbury brought out cake mixes that utilized dried milk and eggs and were so foolproof anyone could bake. When motivational researcher Ernest Dichter discovered bakers hoped to "feel creative" about cakes, mixes were reformulated to call for fresh eggs. By the late 1950s, half the homemade cakes came from mixes.

Refrigerated biscuits, stacked in a can, appeared in 1953. The product was perfected in the 1930s by Lively Willoughby, a Louisville baker, who sold it to Ballard and Ballard Flour Company. When Pillsbury took over Ballard, they introduced "popping" dough to the nation.

In 1950, Kraft created a sensation with already sliced processed cheese; in 1953, they brought out saucy Cheez-Whiz. Both encouraged making sandwiches, grilled and otherwise; cheese consumption rose from 6 to 8 pounds per person between 1940 and 1960.

In May 1954, The American Can Company published this recipe for West Coast Sea Food Supreme using canned tuna, salmon and crabmeat in *Life* magazine. To send for their new cookbook—*Quick Trick Cookery*—only cost fifteen cents.

Fresh from the Freezer

Freezing food to preserve it is an age-old technique, but the defrosted product was limp and off-flavor until the early 1920s when Clarence Birdseye (he pronounced it Bird-see) devised a machine that froze foodstuffs rapidly between two refrigerated metal belts. High speed kept the ice crystals that formed within the food small so they did a minimum of damage to texture. In 1929, Birdseye sold out to Postum Company (later General Foods), which split his surname—and changed the pronunciation.

By the mid-1930s, the label Birds Eye was on almost sixty products ranging from raspberries and asparagus to shrimp and chicken. Home refrigerators, however, had barely enough freezing

New G-E "Book-Shelf" Freezer puts _twice_ as much food within easy reach as a chest freezer!

As frozen foods became standard fare, more freezer space was needed. The model from General Electric advertised in this June 1956 _Look_ ad came in Petal Pink, or five other mix-and-match colors.

Rare Roast Beef

"Prime rib"—actually a U.S. Prime grade beef rib roast—was popular holiday fare before people became concerned about cholesterol. One of the easiest ways to produce ribs that were crusty brown outside and succulent pink inside was developed by Ann Seranne, an editor at _Gourmet_ magazine and a noted cookbook author. She had the butcher remove the short ribs from the beef, then preheated the oven to 500°F, rubbed a little flour and ample salt and pepper into the meat and roasted it for 5 minutes per pound. Without opening the door, she then allowed the beef to rest in the oven for 10 to 20 minutes per pound. (That works out to about 30 minutes roasting and 1 to 2 hours resting for a 4- to 5-pound rib roast.) The problem with this method was that fat spattered the walls and top of the oven. Miss Seranne suggested putting a foil tent over the roast to minimize the mess; using a self-cleaning oven would be even better.

---

space for ice cube trays so cooks could not stock the foods. These were sold by only about six thousand retail grocers nationwide; most frozen products went to restaurants.

After World War II, thrifty families rented frozen-food lockers. The butchers who managed lockers sold wholesale meat at bargain prices and trimmed it to order. Lockers also helped sportsmen, whose fish and game could be professionally cleaned and butchered. Large lockers could be rented to freeze garden products or store-bought frozen food. As sales went up, prices went down, although in the 1950s frozen food was still considered fancy enough to serve to company.

Late in the 1940s, designers increased the freezer space in refrigerators. (Minute Maid frozen orange juice came out in 1947. Cooks wanted to have it on hand.) And in the early 1950s, appliance makers—notably Ben-Hur—produced home freezers. These generally wound up in the basement or on a back porch because they took a lot of space and looked like huge white coffins. But in 1955, Kelvinator showed a side-by-side refrigerator-freezer designed to stand in the kitchen. ("Pack a week's sandwiches for children's lunches," ads suggested, or "Have a supermarket at your elbow.")

Whole precooked meals had been frozen for Army Air Force use in the mid-1940s. Later, small processors froze cooked meals with minor success. But the idea didn't catch on until 1954 when Swanson's introduced its TV dinner. The first one offered turkey, cornbread dressing, peas and sweet potatoes. It was work-free—just heat and eat—and an instant best-seller. Menu variations followed quickly, as did competition.

Baking and Caking

The cook who created original recipes got encouragement from the plethora of competitions. County and state fairs passed out ribbons. Poultry farmers sponsored cook-offs. In San Francisco, Fisherman's Wharf conducted a crab-cooking olympics. The most famous contest was the Pillsbury Bake-Off held in New York's Waldorf-Astoria Hotel in 1949. Officially called the Grand National Recipe and Baking Contest, it was planned as a one-time event, but response was so great that it was repeated yearly during the 1950s.

Even a baker who used cake mixes experimented with pans in fancy shapes: hearts, rings and such. (The first Bundt pan appeared in 1950.) Magazines devoted page after colorful page to showing how cakes could be frosted and trimmed, perhaps cut into pieces and reassembled as a clown or toy train. Decorating kits and food dyes made every cook an *artiste*.

Both chiffon pie and chiffon cake debuted in the 1950s. The pie was credited to Monroe Strause, of Los Angeles, who added beaten egg whites to cream filling until his creation "nearly floated off the table." Chiffon cake— "as light as angel food but as rich as pound cake"—came from Harry Baker of Hollywood, who had made it for movie stars since 1927. When General Mills bought the recipe, his secret ingredient proved to be salad oil. The year they introduced the recipe, their cake flour sales soared 20 percent.

Tuna Fish Pâté

1 small can tuna fish	1/2 teaspoon mustard
1/2 cup butter	cayenne pepper
2 scallions	

In a food blender, combine tuna fish, butter, the white part and a bit of green from scallions, mustard and a pinch of cayenne pepper. Blend just until smooth. Taste for seasoning. Pack the mixture into a small crock or bowl, cover and refrigerate for at least 12 hours to let flavors blend. Makes about 1 cup.

Pork Chops in Wine

One hallmark of sophistication in the 1950s was to cook with wine. These chops are an example.

> 4 1-inch-thick pork chops
> seasoned flour
> 1 tablespoon oil
> 1 teaspoon rosemary
> 1/4 cup white wine or dry sherry

Dust pork chops with seasoned flour. Brown them in oil in a heavy skillet. Pour off excess fat. Sprinkle the chops with rosemary and drizzle white wine or dry sherry over them. Cover the skillet and cook over low heat for about 20 minutes or until they are tender and richly browned. If the chops stick to the skillet during cooking, add a little water to the pan. Serves 4.

The Birth of California Wines

Spanish settlers in Florida were making their own wine in 1565, and Lord Delaware brought vines to Virginia in 1619. Over the years, vintners tried again and again to produce wine that would match that of Europe. Thomas Jefferson attempted to reproduce French varieties from imported vines, but was thwarted by American climate, pests and diseases. Franciscan missionaries to California had little better luck.

The first commercially viable wines came from a mission vineyard in the Sonoma Valley that the Mexican General Mariano Vallejo took over in 1851. Shortly afterward, in 1857, Hungarian-born Agoston Haraszthy came to America to run a Sonoma vineyard; four years later he received state legislature backing for his return to Europe to purchase 100,000 cuttings and collect information on new wine-making techniques. His subsequent success led some to call him "the father of California viticulture." (He dubbed himself "Count.") Lively competition between Vallejo and Haraszthy ended when two of Vallejo's daughters married sons of Haraszthy in a double ceremony.

Serendipitous Sticks

People who caught fish didn't seem to mind cleaning them to get them ready for the table. But non-fishers often disliked the smell and feel of the raw product. Mrs. Paul's Kitchen solved that in 1952 with frozen fish sticks. The fish were chopped, seasoned, shaped into little cylinders and breaded. All the diner had to do was to pop the sticks in a hot oven for 20 minutes or so. Suddenly fish could be part of the menu at home or at school.

Porcupines

Children loved them—and mothers found them easy to make.

1 pound ground beef
1/2 cup fresh bread crumbs
1 egg
1/2 teaspoon salt
pepper
uncooked rice
1 can condensed tomato soup

Combine ground beef, bread crumbs, egg, salt and a grinding of pepper. Shape this mixture into 4 balls and roll them in uncooked rice until coated all over. In a heavy saucepan combine 1 can condensed tomato soup with 1 can water, mix well and bring to a boil. Add the rice-coated balls, cover the pan and simmer for 30 to 40 minutes. Serve the porcupines with the sauce. Serves 4.

Baked Alaska

When refrigerators with ample freezer space became commonplace, housewives could produce this amazing dessert—supposedly named to honor the purchase of Alaska in 1867. Vanilla ice cream is classic, but any flavor might be used.

1-inch-thick layer of sponge cake
1 quart ice cream
6 egg whites
1/2 teaspoon cream of tartar
1/2 cup confectioners' sugar or superfine sugar

Place sponge cake on a small board or ovenproof platter. Soften ice cream slightly, set it on a sheet of waxed paper and mold it to the length and width of the cake. Wrap up the ice cream and freeze it until firm. At serving time, beat egg whites and cream of tartar until soft peaks form; gradually add confectioners' sugar or superfine sugar. Beat until this meringue is stiff and glossy. Unwrap the ice cream, place it on the cake and quickly spread meringue over both. Slide the assembly under a broiler for 2 to 3 minutes or until the meringue begins to brown. Serve at once. Serves 6.

A Changing Larder

War brides from Europe and Asia generally were more eager to learn than to teach, and most of their husbands were wary of "foreign" food. A few seemingly exotic ideas came through: Garlic, squeezed from a press, flavored the butter that chic homemakers slathered on brown-and-serve bread. Oregano was now an essential ingredient of spaghetti sauce. Flavoring foods with wine or beer marinade became commonplace. When temperance-trained cooks looked askance, recipe writers pointed out that the alcoholic content of the marinade boiled away in cooking. (Almost all of it did.)

Some "foreign" food found broader acceptance in American markets: Scottish shortbread, frozen rock lobster tails from South Africa, Dutch cocoa, Chinese tea and Italian Gorgonzola cheese. Yogurt, long sold in Middle Eastern enclaves of big cities, found a wide market in 1947 when Dannon put strawberries in the base of a returnable glass container.

Homogenized fluid milk, at first rejected because of its creamy taste, became standard. Waxed-paper milk cartons had been tried in 1929; depression and war slowed their development. By 1952, though, nearly 40 percent of all milk was being "bottled" in paper instead of breakable glass.

Family Kitchens

The big sellers in early tract developments were ranch-style houses and split-levels, whose open floor plans put no more than partial walls around the kitchen. Homeowners needed to decorate the newly visible kitchens with extra attention. Knotty pine and brick walls brought more color. Plastic laminates brightened countertops, and the floor tiles of vinyl or vinyl-asbestos available in a rainbow of hues could be installed by an ambitious do-it-yourselfer. In 1954, General Electric introduced colored major appliances—blue, pink, yellow and wood-tone brown.

Kitchens were enlarged to provide space for a family to eat and for friends to keep the cook company. Magazines featured kitchens with huge windows and fireplaces. The comfortable chairs and table complemented matching wall cabinets. Television became a must-have.

The modular stove with separate burner and oven units was introduced in 1950—in both gas and electric models. Counters and cabinets were configured to hold the burners and the exhaust fans above them; ovens were recessed in walls or closets. Garbage disposals and dishwashers, which had been launched experimentally in the 1930s, finally became affordable.

New Cookery Gear

Most admired of all utensils were the stainless steel pots with copper bottoms marketed as Revere Ware. They appeared before Pearl Harbor, but not until the late 1940s were families able to get enough of them to put up shining wall displays.

A predictable wedding gift was the fondue pot, a kind of miniature chafing dish. Most cooks used the pot to simmer Swiss cheese and white wine as a dip for cubed French bread, but some discovered they could melt chocolate similarly and dip in pieces of fruit.

Presto's electric skillet took America by storm in 1953. A round "fry pan," it could be set at precise temperatures and never get hotter. The next year H. K. Foster, an engineer for S. W. Farber, Inc., perfected the "probe"—a removable heating element—so an electric skil-

Introduced in 1954, Swanson TV Dinners were an instant hit. Serving a three-course meal in one tray and offering a variety of menus, they were the ultimate in quick and easy cooking. Ad published in *Look* magazine, May 15, 1956.

Home freezers allowed housewives to make meals ahead and freeze them, and also to economize by stocking up on sale items. Another *Look* ad shows a large, chest model, the Kelvinator—"a supermarket at your elbow."

Republic Steel Kitchens!

This is a *different* message about kitchens. The kitchen pictured is different from other kitchens. Look beyond its simple, modern beauty, the well-designed plan for easing kitchen tasks, and you'll find *something more.*

Your Republic Steel Kitchens dealer can duplicate or adapt this modern kitchen plan

Most for your Money!

Only one steel kitchen manufacturer—REPUBLIC—can produce a kitchen line that assures you most for your money. A top quality line at easy-to-budget prices!

Only Republic can give you most for your money because only Republic can guard the quality of its product from raw ore right to your dealer's store.

Republic Steel Kitchens are designed and built by one of the world's greatest steel companies. A pioneer in steel kitchen manufacture. Producers of the kitchen line in which the "extras" are standard!

Don't take our word for it! Compare feature for feature and you'll see, and agree, that you get most for your money when you get Republic Steel Kitchens.

Here's Proof!

Visit your Republic Steel Kitchens dealer. The complete Showdown Comparison chart and a long satisfying look at Republic Steel Kitchens will convince you.

FEATURES	Republic Steel Kitchens	Factory Made Wood Kitchen	Steel Kitchen "A"	Steel Kitchen "B"	Steel Kitchen "C"	Steel Kitchen "D"
TWO-HEIGHT KITCHENS—Installed at the right height for your "comfort reach."	YES	NO	NO	NO	NO	NO
NYLON GLIDES—Offer smooth, quiet drawer operation; no binding.	YES	NO	NO	YES	NO	NO
TOP CLEARANCE RAILS—Between counters and drawers add strength, stop binding.	YES	NO	NO	NO	YES	NO
COVED FORMICA COUNTERS—Continuous smooth surface right up the backsplash.	YES	NO	NO	NO	NO	NO
EASY ACCESS, PULL-OUT CUTTING BOARD—Built in standard cabinet.	YES	NO				

You'll want these idea booklets if you're remodeling or building
Check those you want, and enclose necessary coin for handling and mailing. One booklet, 25 cents; two for 40 cents, three for 50 cents. Address: Republic Steel Kitchens, Department A, 1058 Belden Avenue, Canton 5, Ohio. 1-245
☐ For remodelers, "101 Ways To Make An Award Kitchen Behave"
☐ For new home builders, "Prize-Winning Kitchens"
☐ "How Mary and I Installed Our Own Republic Kitchen"

Name _____
Address _____ County _____
City _____ Zone ___ State ___

REPUBLIC STEEL Kitchens   *The World's Most Modern Kitchens*

In this 1954 ad from *Life,* the sleek look of a stainless steel kitchen with Formica counter tops shows the changing concept of kitchens. With the open-interior design of ranch houses, it was important that the kitchen be decorated as nicely as the rest of the house.

Spinach-Bacon Salad

During the 1950s, iceberg lettuce fell out of favor and fresh spinach greens became stylish.

    1 pound spinach leaves
    3 slices of bacon cut into 1-inch pieces
    1/4 cup olive oil
    1/4 cup wine vinegar
    1 teaspoon sugar
    black pepper

Tear off stems and blemishes from freshly washed spinach leaves. Pat leaves dry, tear them into small pieces and drop them into a salad bowl. Sauté the bacon pieces until crisp. Drain the bacon. Pour off the bacon fat from the skillet and add olive oil. Return the bacon and stir over high heat for a few seconds. Off the heat, add wine vinegar and sugar. Stir well, then pour the mixture over the spinach. Season with several grindings of black pepper. Serves 2.

---

let could be submerged in water for washing. Soon there were electric saucepans, deep fryers, even woks. To show off the spit in its electric table broiler, Rotissomat Corporation set up demonstrations in poultry stores. Descendants of those birds still turn on spits in delicatessens across the country.

Carried away by their creativity, manufacturers devised electric egg-timers, chafing dishes, bean pots, and popcorn poppers. The Thanksgiving turkey was portioned ceremoniously with an electric carving knife. For can-opener cooks, the most useful device must have been the electric can opener introduced by Udico in 1956. Within months, seven other free-standing and wall-mounted versions appeared.

Plastics developed during the war and shortly thereafter provided the cook with breakproof urea formaldehyde Melamine dishes, flexible polyethylene Tupperware food storage containers and clinging polyvinylidene chloride Saran Wrap. In 1953, Dr. Donald Stookey of Corning Glass created a glass-ceramic for use as the nose cone of a missile for NASA. This white Pyroceram reached consumers five years later as pans and dishes that could go straight from the freezer to a hot oven without breaking.

Pressure cookers were the rage. A working pressure cooker, called a Digester, was invented in the 1680s by French chef Denis Papin. However, it was hard to regulate and caused explosions, so the Digester was pretty much forgotten until 1811. Then, to win a prize from Napoleon Bonaparte ("An army marches on its stomach"), Nicholas Appert invented canning by reworking Papin's ideas.

In 1917, the USDA had determined that pressure canners were necessary to process low-acid foods. But these vessels were heavy and dangerous until 1938 when Alfred Vischer, Jr. made his Flex-Seal models—some for preserving, some for daily use. Sales soared, then the military ordered all he could produce. After the war, housewives hurried to buy them as timesavers. Competitors rushed into the business. In his chronicle of the housewares industry, Earl Lifshey says eighty-five makers flooded the market with different versions. Sadly, some were unsafe, accidents occurred and, again, pressure cookers were banished.

The old-time pop-up toaster had been refined by 1947 to lower bread automatically, toast it to the desired color, then eject it. Waring's Blendor also was born again in the 1940s, with ice crushing and coffee grinding attachments. Still, the Blendor's image was that of a drink mixer—and no cocktail party was complete without frozen daiquiris.

Chocolate Fondue

1/2 cup cream
2 tablespoons rum or bourbon
8 ounces chocolate chips or milk chocolate
pear cubes, banana slices, pineapple chunks, strawberries

At the serving table, heat cream in a fondue pot over a high flame. Add rum or bourbon. Stir in chocolate chips or milk chocolate, broken into small pieces. Spear one pear cube, banana slice, pineapple chunk or strawberry at a time on a fondue fork or small skewer and swirl it in the chocolate mixture.

Oven-Fried Fish Fillets

Oven-frying became a quick and tidy substitute for deep-frying fish as well as chicken during the busy 1950s.

1 pound fish fillets
1/2 cup milk
soft bread crumbs
salt, pepper, and paprika
2 tablespoons oil or melted butter
parsley and lemon wedges (garnish)

Dip fish fillets—thawed and patted dry if frozen—one at a time into a bowl holding milk. Roll each fillet in soft bread crumbs seasoned with salt, pepper and a little paprika. Let fillets dry on a wire rack for 15 minutes so the coating becomes firm, then place them in an oiled or buttered baking/serving dish and sprinkle them with oil or melted butter. Bake at 350°F for about 15 minutes or until the fish feels firm when pressed lightly. Garnish with parsley and lemon wedges. Serves 4.

Supermarketing

The wicker basket on wheels that Sylvan Goldman invented in Oklahoma City in 1937 had been transmogrified into a metal shopping cart and improved a dozen times—as had the market where it was used. About one-third of all grocery business went to supermarkets in 1950, two-thirds in 1960. Bulk buying let even small chains undersell neighborhood grocers.

During the early 1940s when wartime shortages led to empty shelves, markets filled the space with whatever merchandise they could find: toiletries, proprietary drugs, stationery and such. After V-day, most continued to sell them. Average supermarkets held about 5,600 items in twenty thousand square feet.

Trading Stamps

During the 1950s, supermarkets issued millions of trading stamps to lure customers. The biggest stamp distributor was Sperry Hutchinson, which started peddling S&H green stamps in 1896.

For the shopper, stamps meant something for nothing—markets doled out one stamp for each dime spent. Shoppers pasted stamps into books holding twelve hundred and cashed in books

Italian Coffee Cream

1/4 cup heavy cream	1 tablespoon instant coffee
3 cups ricotta cheese	1 tablespoon brandy
1/4 cup superfine sugar	

Beat cream into ricotta cheese. Add superfine sugar, instant coffee and brandy. Taste and add more sugar, if desired. Cover tightly and refrigerate for at least 1 hour. Serves 4.

for merchandise from the stamp company catalog or, in big cities, stamp redemption centers. Each book represented $120 worth of purchases, but its redemption value was $3, so a shopper needed a pocketful to get a valuable prize.

Stamps cost about 2 percent of gross sales, so many markets refused to carry them. Nonetheless, by 1959, some 75 percent of American families saved stamps.

Cooking Lessons and Recipes

Both James Beard and Dione Lucas, who were already known to a savvy audience for their cookbooks, appeared on television early. Beard was featured on NBC weekly from August 1946 to May 1947; Lucas appeared on CBS weekly from October 1947 to December 1949. Sadly, in 1946 only about eight thousand families had sets, and pictures were in black-and-white. By 1960, the total was

Poppy Cannon, author of *The Can-Opener Cookbook,* hosted a TV cooking show on NBC, showing busy women how to whip up elegant dishes from canned, frozen and instant foods.

forty-six million, but color television sets were expensive and rare because of their price. The first color sets from RCA in 1954 cost $1,000.

Cooks got recipes and advice from papers and magazines, package inserts and grocery store demonstrators. Advertisers offered cookbooks free. Serious cooks found a variety of book titles—forty-nine published in 1960 alone. Beard himself wrote more than half a dozen, including the beautiful best-seller *The Fireside Cook Book* in 1949 and *The James Beard Cookbook* ten years later. *Gourmet* magazine published its first recipe collection in 1950 for the shockingly high price of $10; *Betty Crocker's Cookbook* appeared that year for only $2.95–$3.95 in a loose-leaf binder. *Better Homes*

& *Gardens* claimed its cookbook was outselling the Bible.

Poppy Cannon, who wrote for *Mademoiselle* and *Cosmopolitan* magazines, took a gourmet approach in her 1951 *The Can-Opener Cookbook*. "Armed with a can-opener, I become the artist-cook, the master, the creative chef." True to her word, she made lobster thermidor, paella a la Valenciana and similar classics from canned, frozen, dehydrated and otherwise packaged products. She duked up canned stew with herbs and wine, flamed a canned ham and combined condensed tomato soup, grated Cheddar and eggs for a soufflé.

Bananas Foster

During the 1950s, Chef Paul Blange of Brennan's restaurant in New Orleans created this fanciful flaming dessert for a favored customer.

4 tablespoons butter	4 bananas
1/4 cup brown sugar	1/4 cup rum
cinnamon	4 portions vanilla ice cream
1/4 cup banana-flavored liqueur	

Melt butter in the shallow top pan of a chafing dish set over a medium flame. Stir in brown sugar and a generous sprinkling of cinnamon. Add banana-flavored liqueur. Cut bananas in half lengthwise, then again in half crosswise. Place the bananas in the pan and sauté them until they are soft. Add rum; when it is warmed, ignite it. After the flames die down, spoon the bananas onto 4 portions of vanilla ice cream and pour the sauce over them. Serves 4.

Chapter Nine
An Epicure Is Born (1960–1980)

*M*ore Americans than ever went to college and bought homes, cars and boats in the 1960s and 1970s. They glimpsed other countries' culinary traditions at the 1964 New York World's Fair, then explored first-hand as planes got bigger and fares smaller. In 1970, close to five million flew or sailed overseas.

Food indicated status. Knowing about a spectrum of foreign cuisines now called "ethnic" became the mark of a cultivated person. Cooking was stylish and increasingly sophisticated. After decades of make-it-do shortcuts, Americans were ready to prepare foods from scratch—at least on weekends when they had time to spare.

The frozen TV dinner was more than an easy solution to dinner, it also effected social changes, most notably to dinnertime conversation. People now started watching television while they ate, as spoofed here in a drawing by Constantin Alajalov.

The Lady of the House

Despite Betty Friedan's 1963 *The Feminine Mystique*, most housewives considered themselves homebodies. Fewer than 40 percent of women had a job outside the home that year. With their boom babies now in school, some mothers found cookery an outlet for artistic energy. Julia Child's "The French Chef" on public television charmed viewers, and she was their "pied piper" into the world of gourmet food. The 1963 show won such admiration that it was high praise indeed, a few years later, to call Joyce Chen "the Chinese Julia Child." In 1969, Graham Kerr, a handsome Englishman who learned to cook in Australia, became daytime TV's "Galloping Gourmet." The audience he cajoled away from soap opera felt heartbroken when he retired in 1973.

The next year marked a watershed in women's liberation. More women worked (by a ratio of 52 to 48 percent) than stayed home.

Canny Cookery

Andy Warhol's 1962 painting of a Campbell's tomato soup can was an appropriate metaphor for contemporary food. Women depended on cans and boxes to put three meals a day together for such members of the family as appeared at the communal table. Increasingly, children and parents had different schedules and ate separately, preparing individual dishes—here TV dinners were a blessing—or heating leftovers.

Avgolemono Soup

4 cups chicken stock	2 tablespoons lemon juice
1/3 cup rice	sliced lemons (garnish)
2 eggs	

Combine chicken stock and rice in a heavy pan. Bring to a boil, reduce the heat and simmer for 15 to 20 minutes. When the rice is tender, remove the pan from the heat to cool. In a bowl, whisk eggs until thick and pale yellow. Add lemon juice. Whisk vigorously while slowly pouring about 1 cup of hot stock into the eggs. Whisk this mixture into the pan of soup; it will thicken slightly. Refrigerate for 3 hours. Garnish with sliced lemons. Serves 4.

Frozen foods proliferated, especially fully cooked ones like meat pies, fish sticks and the tacos, pizza and chow mein that were no longer considered foreign. Rice-A-Roni, the "San Francisco treat," went national in 1961. General Foods' Tang appeared in 1965 and landed on the moon with the astronauts in 1969. Another 1965 first was the popular canned product that Franco-American called Spaghetti-Os, "O-shaped spaghetti kids can eat with a spoon." In 1970, General Mills brought out Hamburger Helper in five flavors; these sold so well that two years later, they added Tuna Helper.

Something Special for Guests

Paradoxically, entertaining at home grew less slapdash. When company was coming, cooks prided themselves on making every dish—soup to tarts—from scratch. In their enthusiasm for

Selecting frozen vegetables from the freezer section of a supermarket, a shopper had hundreds of varieties and brands to choose from. This photo was taken at a store in Kensington, Maryland, in 1965.

By 1968, when this photo was taken, as more women joined the work force and many families had two working parents, quick meals became more crucial to harried housewives, like the one shown here putting an entire meal together from prepackaged foods.

Continental cuisine, Americans outdid Europeans, who rarely attempted to bake breads or stuff sausages at home.

Inviting guests to dinner provided an excuse to show off culinary achievements, and a housewife who planned ahead could serve three courses comfortably: stuffed artichoke hearts, veal scallops with Marsala sauce, cheesecake. If she wanted to try her hand at fancier fare—beef Wellington, puff pastry desserts—she could join a gourmet club where each member would contribute one triumphant dish to a lavishly orchestrated menu.

Elegant food was served in an appropriately handsome setting. A damask or lace cloth, bone china, crystal goblets and sterling silver appeared on tables that had held placemats, plastic dishes, restaurant glasses and stainless steel flatware just a decade earlier.

Informal entertaining still centered around the barbecue grill if weather was pleasant. Otherwise, hostesses favored buffet suppers, or cocktail parties with finger foods displayed buffet style. Cocktail-party bars offered wine and bottled water as fashions in drinking changed. Mixed drinks based on wine—Byrrh, spritzers, vermouth cassis—replaced old-time highballs.

Diana's Cheesecake

1 pound cream cheese, softened	4 eggs
1 pound cottage cheese	1/4 cup cornstarch
2 cups sour cream	2 tablespoons flour
1/2 cup cooled melted butter	1 tablespoon vanilla extract
1-1/2 cups superfine sugar	cherry or blueberry sauce (optional)

Beat together softened cream cheese, cottage cheese, sour cream and melted butter. When the mixture is smooth, beat in sugar. Add eggs, one at a time. Then stir in cornstarch, flour and vanilla extract. Pour into a greased 9-inch springform pan. Bake at 350°F for one hour or until the cake is firm around the edges. Turn off the oven and let the cake cool there for at least two hours. Chill the cake. To serve, run a spatula around the inside of the pan, then release its clasps and leave the cake on the bottom of the pan. Accompany with cherry or blueberry sauce, if desired.

By the 1970s, hostesses were calling raw vegetables they served with dips *crudités*—and added mushrooms and fennel to the celery-carrot mix.

The Gourmet Invasion

Advertising—and table conversation—turned so often to gourmet-that and gourmet-this most cooks began to agree with James Beard: "The word gourmet has been run into the ground. Anybody's cousin who drinks wine with his meals or who substitutes broccoli for potatoes considers himself a gourmet." He preferred "epicure ... a man who likes food (whereas) a gourmet likes talking about food."

Whatever its characterization, food underwent more fashion changes than hemlines did. During the 1960s, French dishes like *coq au vin* and *boeuf bourguignon* were "in"; by the 1970s, cooks ventured farther with North Italian *osso buco* and Japanese *sukiyaki* or Greek *moussaka*. Herbs, which early settlers took for granted, had been long forgotten; now they were chic. Watercress or parsley (preferably flat-leaf or Italian parsley) seemed to garnish every course except dessert. French foods were dosed

A growing interest in gourmet foods naturally led to a growing interest in wines. Here a customer listens to a description of a wine's vintage, its body and bouquet, at a wine and cheese shop in Washington, D.C. in 1965. The sophisticated epicure had some knowledge of wines.

Carbonnade

3 large onions, sliced	1 cup beef stock
oil	1 bay leaf
2 pounds beef	2 teaspoons thyme
flour	salt and pepper
2 tablespoons brown sugar	dumplings, boiled potatoes
2 cups beer	or noodles

Cook onions in oil in a heavy skillet over low heat until they are soft and lightly caramelized. Pour them into a sieve set over a bowl to drain. Dust beef, sliced 1/4 inch thick, with flour. Pour about 1 tablespoon oil into the skillet and brown a few slices at a time. Add oil by the spoonful as needed. As the beef is browned, put the slices in a 6-quart casserole in layers alternated with the onions. Finally, add brown sugar to the skillet and stir over low heat until it melts. Stir in beer and beef stock; bring to a boil. Add bay leaf, thyme and salt and pepper to the casserole. Pour in the beer mixture, cover and bake at 325°F for 2 hours or until the beef is tender. Serve with dumplings, boiled potatoes or noodles. Serves 4 to 6.

with thyme and rosemary; Italian foods carried basil in addition to oregano. Coriander was called either Chinese parsley or Mexican *cilantro*, depending on which cuisine it flavored. After decades of temperance and shortages, wines could be used generously to flavor sauces and desserts. Brandy flamed crepes or cherries.

Iceberg lettuce was considered passé. Salad favorites of the 1960s were Bibb and Boston lettuce, spinach, dandelion, rocket (*arugula*) and red chicory (*radicchio*). Caesar salad, with its romaine leaves, garlic croutons and anchovy fillets, swept across the country from California. During the 1970s, stylish cooks discovered sorrel, lamb's quarter and fiddlehead fern.

As African Americans' pride grew with slogans like "Black Is Beautiful," dishes once rejected as reminders of slavery were revived as soul food. Chitterlings, collard greens and sweet-potato pie

A Hispanic grocery store advertises meats and fruits in Spanish. In 1965, a change in immigration quotas brought about an influx of Latin Americans as well as Asians. Ethnic markets reflected the changing demographics.

Regional cooking came back into vogue, although not limited to its region of origin. These sweet potato pies, a traditional Southern dessert, were made in a bakery in New Jersey. Photo by David Taylor.

Black pride revived an interest in soul food, which included dishes such as chitterlings, collard greens and black-eyed peas.

became the first nostalgic "comfort foods." The Bicentennial celebrations of 1976 revived interest in regional cookery.

In 1965, the national-origin immigration quotas were abolished. Asians and Latin Americans quickly took advantage of the change—and brought culinary ideas from countries as far away as Korea and Argentina, Japan and Chile. Mexico contributed to the melting pot; so did the Caribbean islands, especially Puerto Rico and Cuba.

Nouvelle Cuisine

In 1972, French food critics Henri Gault and Christian Millau pronounced *grande cuisine* obsoleted by *nouvelle cuisine*, which treated the finest ingredients "honestly" to produce superior food. Historians believe that Chef Fernand Point of La Pyramide restaurant in Vienne, France, actually began the revolution during the 1940s by lightening classic dishes and rich sauces.

Paul Bocuse, who apprenticed with Point, had opened his own restaurant near Lyons in 1962. There he sauced with reduced pan drippings or butter; he undercooked fish and poultry slightly to preserve their juices; he left a crunch in vegetables. Soon other remarkable French chefs, Alain Chapel, Jean and Pierre Troisgros and Roger Vergé among them, allied with him. Bocuse became a spokesman for *nouvelle* chefs, writing cookbooks and traveling to America and Japan to teach. Michel Guérard added *cuisine minceur*, "the cookery of slimness." He baked, poached or steamed foods, using herbs to replace butter, cream or oil. Guérard banished sugars, except those of fruit. He sought miniature vegetables and became a culinary artist in arranging foods on a plate.

American chefs quickly gave *nouvelle cuisine* a twist to create American *nouvelle* or California cuisine: local foods cooked—preferably grilled over mesquite—until barely done and sauced with meat stock reduced to syrup, spicy tomato *salsa* or *creme fraiche*. Innovators in America were led by Alice Waters, the "Mother of New American Cuisine," and chefs who worked with her at Chez Panisse, her Berkeley restaurant—Jeremiah Tower, Jonathan Waxman, Joyce Goldstein and Mark Miller among them. Because the Californians depended on minimum cooking, the quality of ingredients assumed maximum importance. Locally grown pro-

duce and locally caught fish and shellfish were essential for freshness. Guerard's lessons about food's appearance led to dishes being as beautiful as they were delicious.

Edna Lewis, affectionately known as The First Lady of Southern Cooking, put the same stress on natural ingredients—even insisting on organically grown lemons. As a professional chef, Lewis introduced gumbo to New York City and her special beef brisket to Charleston.

Bigger Larder

Almost all formerly seasonal foods were now available year-round. Leeks and shallots developed into staples. When Asian, Caribbean and Latin American immigrants became farmers—and customers—supermarkets displayed daikon, bamboo shoots, plantain, snow peas and kumquats.

In 1962, Frieda Caplan established a produce specialty business in Los Angeles, selling California brown mushrooms labeled "Frieda's Finest" nationwide. Over the years, she introduced kiwi fruit, spaghetti squash, purple potatoes and cactus pears. W. Atlee Burpee's 1979 seed catalog heralded Dr. Calvin Lamborn's sugar snap pea, a plumper, sweeter snow pea. Adding to its cachet, it was a fashion statement only gardeners could make!

America's love affair with beef reached its apogee in 1976, when per person consumption reached 94.4 pounds. That same year, the Department of Agriculture set new grading standards. Among other changes, these reduced the amount of marbling (veins of fat) required for

---

Chilies Rellenos con Queso

1/4 pound Monterey Jack cheese	4 eggs, separated
8 canned peeled green chilies	1/4 cup flour
	oil
flour	salsa

Cut Monterey Jack cheese into 8 sticks, each about 1/2 inch thick and 1 inch long. Wrap the sticks in canned peeled green chilies. Roll one chili at a time in flour, then dip it in batter made by combining egg whites, beaten until stiff, with yolks that have been beaten with flour. As each chili is dipped, slide it from a saucer into a deep pot containing about 1 inch of oil heated to 375°F. Use a spoon to baste the chili with oil. When golden brown, drain it on absorbent paper. Serve with salsa. Serves 4.

Coquilles St. Jacques

The French translation of scallops is *coquilles*, an elegant term bestowed in America on this fancy concoction.

1-1/2 pounds scallops	4 tablespoons butter
1-1/2 cups dry white wine	flour
1/2 cup chopped shallots or onions	3 egg yolks
4 parsley sprigs	1/2 cup cream
1 bay leaf	salt, red pepper, lemon juice
1/2 teaspoon thyme	1/4 cup grated Gruyère or Parmesan cheese
1/2 pound fresh mushrooms, chopped	

Combine scallops, white wine, shallots or onions, parsley sprigs, bay leaf and thyme in a saucepan. Cook for about 5 minutes until the scallops are opaque and firm. Strain the liquid into a small pan and boil it down to 1 cup. Meanwhile, cut the scallops into halves if large. Sauté chopped fresh mushrooms in 2 tablespoons butter for about 5 minutes. Drain and add them to the scallops. Melt the 2 remaining tablespoons butter in a saucepan and stir in flour. Mix in the reduced scallop stock. Beat egg yolks with cream and slowly stir this mixture into the simmering sauce; cook until the sauce is thick. Off the heat season to taste with salt, red pepper and lemon juice. Stir in the scallops and mushrooms. Spoon the combination into 8 scallop shells or ramekins. Sprinkle the tops with grated Gruyère or Parmesan cheese. Broil 6 inches from the heat until golden brown. Serves 8.

prime and choice beef, thus multiplying the number of steers eligible for such distinction. Cattlemen applauded, but diners worried.

Turkey growers promoted the bird year-round, and annual sales reached about 10 pounds per person in 1980. That year sales of chickens—some with brand names—flew to 50 pounds per person.

Coffee and dessert were a snap with instant coffee, pie from a box and whipped cream in a can, as shown in this 1965 photo.

Changes at the Bar

Carbonated water and mineral water had been sold in upscale markets for generations. During the 1970s, they became voguish, especially if imported, and appeared at cocktail time and on the dinner table as sober substitutes for wine or spirits.

Wine sales nearly tripled. Wine tastings were a popular home entertainment. As vineyards increased, so did American wines—about two-thirds from California. At first these were blends or "generics" with names such as Mountain Red, or they copied European wines. But by the 1970s, vintners were creating unique "varietals" named for grapes they contained—Pinot Noir or Zinfandel, for example.

The most popular distilled drink was vodka, essential for the omnipresent bloody Marys. It overtook gin for martinis. In 1979, it outsold gin two to one and bourbon, about five to four.

A barrage of advertising reminded Americans of local beers; imports grew increasingly available. Light beers—promising enjoyment without intoxication or obesity—proved a sensation. Total beer sales rose from 15 to 24 gallons per capita.

In 1976, carbonated soft drinks replaced coffee as the chief between-meals pick-me-up. In 1980, bottlers sold 34 gallons per capita—about 8 ounces of root beer, cola or fruit drink daily for every man, woman and child.

Buttered Radishes

The French serve fresh radishes topped with a bit of butter—a pleasing contrast. Being an artist as well as a cook, Carol Cutler took the idea a step farther:

3 cups red radishes	2 tablespoons butter
boiling, salted water	2 tablespoons lemon juice

Trim radishes. Drop them into boiling salted water and cook for 15 minutes until barely tender. Drain off the water. Add butter and lemon juice to the pan. Season. Serves 3 or 4.

Bigger and Better Kitchens

The dream kitchen held a dining area and—as an increasing number of men took cooking more seriously—enough counter space so husband and wife could work side by side. To meet both aims, an "island" of cabinets was set in the center of the room. Often one side offered work space; the other served as a dining counter.

The name Manna Oriental Foods may well reflect the owner's belief that food is a spiritual nourishment as well as a physical requirement.

The shelves of a Korean grocery are crowded with exotic foods. Here one might buy sea-weed, ginseng root or pickled eel.

Many American desserts have their roots in German and Danish recipes.

Scampi

24 jumbo shrimp	2 garlic cloves, minced
1/2 cup olive oil	parsley (garnish)
1/4 cup melted butter	

With scissors, cut almost to the tail along the outside curve of shrimp, thus splitting the shell while keeping it in place. Remove the sand veins. Combine olive oil, melted butter and minced garlic cloves. Dip the shrimp in the oil mixture and stand them in a baking dish. Drizzle the remaining oil over the shrimp. Broil them 6 to 8 inches from the heat for about 10 minutes or until their flesh is firm and cooked through. Garnish with chopped parsley and serve them from the baking dish. Serves 4 to 6.

Barbecued Spareribs, Chinese Style

1/2 cup soy sauce	1 tablespoon minced fresh
1/2 cup dry sherry	ginger
1/2 cup water	2 garlic cloves, minced
4 tablespoons brown sugar	4 pounds spareribs

In a large baking dish, combine soy sauce, sherry, water, brown sugar, minced fresh ginger and garlic cloves. Add spareribs; turn them to coat them evenly with the soy mixture. Cover the dish with foil and marinate the ribs in the refrigerator for at least 12 hours. Bake at 350°F for 1 hour, turning the ribs once. Then barbecue them over coals or broil them in the oven—6 to 8 inches from the heat for about 30 minutes, basting them with marinade and turning them once or twice. Serves 6.

Shrimp Jambalaya

1 tablespoon olive oil	1 pound fresh or frozen
2–3 cloves garlic, minced	shrimp, cleaned
1 green pepper, chopped	2 cups water
1 medium onion, chopped fine	1/2 teaspoon salt or to taste
1 16-ounce can whole tomatoes, chopped	1/4 teaspoon thyme
	1/8 teaspoon pepper
1 tablespoon Worcestershire sauce	1/4–1/2 teaspoon cayenne
1 cup uncooked long-grain rice	pepper or to taste

Cut up green pepper and onion as indicated above. Heat olive oil in heavy 10-inch skillet. Add minced garlic, green pepper and onion. Sauté 5 minutes. Add chopped tomatoes and Worcestershire sauce to skillet. Thaw shrimp, if frozen, and drain. Add shrimp to skillet along with water and seasonings. Bring to a boil. Stir in rice. As soon as mixture returns to a boil, reduce heat. Simmer, covered, about 30 minutes or until all liquid is absorbed.

For a variation, substitute 2 to 3 cups cooked chicken or turkey meat. Another delicious variation is to use 1/2 pound shrimp and 1/2 pound scallops. Corn bread provides a nice complement to this meal.

Recipe courtesy of Janet M. Chiavetta, from *Eat, Drink and Be Healthy* (Fulcrum Publishing, 1995).

In any arrangement, the kitchen became automated. At the start of the 1960s, only 7 percent of homes had a dishwasher and 11 percent, a garbage disposal; by 1980, those numbers leapt to 43 and 62 percent. In 1963, General Electric developed self-cleaning ovens; in 1965, Frigidaire introduced a refrigerator with an ice maker in the door; in 1969, Whirlpool showed the trash compactor.

During World War II, Dr. Percy L. Spencer, a scientist with the electronics manufacturer Raytheon, discovered that he could pop corn speedily with microwaves. Popcorn was just the start of a culinary revolution. After the war, Raytheon sold restaurant-sized microwave ovens about 5 feet tall, weighing 750 pounds, and costing $3,000. Prices gradually decreased along with sizes, but microwave ovens did not become practical home appliances until 1967 when Amana, a Raytheon division, produced a 115-volt countertop model for $495.

During the 1970s, however, the stove most coveted by knowledgeable cooks was the huge gas restaurant range with six or more burners, two ovens and a broiler that reached 700°F—or higher.

The appliance on almost every cook's wish list was the Cuisinart food processor. Other multipurpose devices required a drawerful of attachments; this one had two disks for shredding and slicing and two blades for cutting, pureeing and mixing. Made in France, it was brought to America—after some redesigning for user safety—by Carl Sontheimer. He introduced it in 1973 at $175, tempting competitors to bring out cheaper versions. Yet in 1977 when all makes sold half a million, half were Cuisinart.

A balloon whisk and copper bowl for beating egg whites and a European-made chef's knife for chopping vegetables were hallmarks of dedication. Copper pots were displayed proudly on kitchen walls. Although restaurant suppliers of such gear had little patience with amateurs, the demands grew. *The Cook's Catalogue* in 1975 was 565 pages long; *The International Cook's Catalogue* of 1977 ran 431 pages. To supply amateurs, new "serious" kitchenware stores like La Cuisine in Alexandria, Virginia, opened. Old ones like Williams-Sonoma in San Francisco expanded.

Health conscious consumers, like this woman photographed in 1973, started forgoing prepackaged, processed foods in favor of fresh fruits and vegetables and non-meat sources of protein such as eggs or tofu, a soybean product.

Recipes and Reviews

With sophistication came a heightened desire for information. The paradigm for food reportage was *The New York Times*, which hired Craig Claiborne, the first male food editor, in 1957. He supplied recipes, reviewed restaurants and interviewed local and visiting chefs. Claiborne focused on Manhattan, but he also traveled across the nation and around the world ferreting out food news.

Three food magazines debuted. *Bon Appetit* appeared in 1975 from Knapp Communications. In 1978, Carl Sontheimer of Cuisinart brought out *Cooking*, soon renamed *The Pleasures of Cooking*. Aline and Michael Batterberry started *The International Review of Food & Wine* in 1978; publication stopped in 1979, then resumed in 1980 as *Food & Wine* after American Express bought it.

Cookbooks sold by the tens of thousands as cooks collected and read them for pleasure as well as recipes. Nineteen sixty-one was a banner year with *Mastering the Art of French Cooking* by Louisette Bertholle, Simone Beck and Julia Child and a 1101-page American edition of *Larousse Gastronomique*, the French cook's bible. In 1968, Time-Life Books launched the *Foods of the World*, a seminal series of twenty-seven volumes covering foods from all parts of the globe and regions of the United States. Instead of tempering ethnic cuisines to American tastes, *Foods of the World* set high standards with authentic recipes from native chefs.

In 1969 there were more than twelve hundred cookbooks in print. Hundreds of new titles

Cassata Siciliana

1-1/2 pounds ricotta	1/4 cup finely diced candied
1/2 cup superfine sugar	fruit, plus 2–3
4 tablespoons rum	tablespoons for garnish
1/2 cup chopped roasted	1 square unsweetened
almonds	chocolate, grated
1 loaf pound cake	1 cup heavy cream

Beat ricotta, sugar and 1 tablespoon rum together in a bowl until light and fluffy. Stir in almonds, candied fruit and unsweetened chocolate. Cut a loaf of pound cake crosswise into three layers. Place the bottom layer on a serving plate and sprinkle it with 1 tablespoon rum, spread one half of the ricotta mixture on the cake. Repeat with the second layer. Set the third layer on top and sprinkle it with 1 tablespoon rum. Wrap the cake in foil and refrigerate it for at least 3 hours to let the flavors blend. Before serving, whip cream and spread it over the top and sides of the cake. Sprinkle 2 or 3 tablespoons of diced fruit over the whipped cream. Serves 8.

Developed in the 1940s, the microwave oven debuted as a home appliance in 1967. Cutting cooking times down from hours to minutes, it became an indispensable fixture in the majority of American kitchens.

appeared every year, making cook-books big business. Although many volumes might aptly be called "pot-boilers," author James Beard wrote better than ever and was joined by others such as Bernard Clayton, Richard Olney, Michael Field, Jacques Pepin, Edna Lewis, George Lang and Marcella Hazan.

Cooking Schools

Suddenly, or so it seemed, every town had at least one private school teaching the culinary arts to hobbyists. Metropolitan areas had dozens of schools. Some concentrated on special techniques like bread-making or cake decorating. Some devoted attention to one cuisine—French, Italian or Mexican, for example—and students found most countries had regional or provincial food differences. To set standards, Francois Dionot, who was director of L'Academie de Cuisine in Bethesda, Maryland, organized the Association of Cooking Schools in 1978. By 1984, it had twelve hundred members.

Chef Francois Dionot teaches a cooking class at L'Academie de Cuisine in Bethesda, Maryland in 1981. Cooking schools proliferated as people wanted to learn about myriad international and regional cuisines as well as cooking styles and techniques.

Super Supermarkets

The inventory of a supermarket—now figured in SKUs or stock keeping units—exploded to ninety-four hundred items by 1980. Selling space averaged 20,000 square feet. Check-out clerks used scanners—at first hand-held, then recessed in counters—to read the bar codes manufacturers printed on processed foods and yield itemized word-plus-price receipts for shoppers.

In 1967, three out of four markets offered trading stamps worth $825 million—more than twice the total for 1956. Even A&P and Safeway, which had held out against the trend, gave away stamps.

Jack Hooley found an alternative to stamps in 1968 when he opened a "warehouse store" in Minneapolis. He under-sold his competition by dispens-

A far cry from the days when early settlers eked out an existence from the land, modern supermarkets carry as many as thirty-five thousand different products, including beauty care products, stationery, household items and automotive parts.

Smart shoppers not only compare prices, but also check labels for the nutritional charts now required by law to list calories, fat, carbohydrate and protein content per serving.

ing with service except for meat, leaving canned and boxed goods in cartons and produce in bushel baskets. He made no effort to stock every size or flavor. He expected customers to compromise and to bag their own groceries—paying for each bag. To encourage them to save (i.e., buy) more, he got bigger carts. Other grocers followed suit.

By the 1970s, shoppers had grown tired of collecting stamps. Markets concentrated on manufacturers' coupons distributed by mail and in newspapers and food packages. Coupons rewarded shoppers with instant savings, some with money back, more allowing money off retail prices. Markets held double- and triple-coupon days—raising the ante. Bright-eyed shoppers set up a cottage industry to sell coupon holders, newsletters, even "how-to use coupons" books.

Natural Foods and Farms

In the late 1960s, young men and women joined farm communes to "get back to nature." Most communes closed within a year or so, but ex-members patronized stores selling organic produce—even if the apples and corn were wormy. And these social rebels put out counterculture publications

Curried Chicken

4 skinned, boneless	2 teaspoons curry powder
chicken breast halves	1/2 teaspoon salt
flour	1-1/2 cups chicken stock
2 tablespoons butter	2 cups sour cream
1/4 cup chopped onion	boiled rice
1 cup chopped apple	

Cube chicken breasts, dust with flour and sauté in butter until lightly browned. Stir in chopped onion, apple, curry powder and salt. Add chicken stock. Mix well. Bring to a boil, reduce heat, cover and simmer for 10 minutes. Add 2 cups sour cream and simmer uncovered for 10 minutes longer or until sauce is thick and bubbly. Taste for seasoning. Serve with boiled rice. Serves 4.

Carrot Cake

1-1/2 cups sugar	3/4 cup skim milk
1-1/2 cups all-purpose flour	1/2 cup natural applesauce
1 cup whole wheat flour	2 teaspoons vanilla
1-1/2 teaspoons baking soda	3/4 cup boiling water
1-1/2 teaspoons baking powder	2 cups finely shredded carrots
1/2 teaspoon salt	(2 to 3 carrots)
2 teaspoons cinnamon	1 teaspoon allspice
4 egg whites	

Cream Cheese Frosting:

3 ounces light cream cheese	2 cups powdered sugar
1 tablespoon tub margarine	3 tablespoons chopped walnuts
1 teaspoon vanilla	

Preheat oven to 375°F. Grate carrots. Set aside. Combine sugar, flours, baking soda, baking powder, salt, cinnamon and allspice in a large mixing bowl. Blend together well. To same mixing bowl, add egg whites, milk, applesauce, vanilla and boiling water. Beat at high speed for 2 minutes. Fold in grated carrots. Spray 10-inch bundt pan with vegetable cooking spray. Pour in batter. Bake at 375°F 40 to 50 minutes or until toothpick inserted in center comes out clean. Remove from oven and cool slightly. Loosen edges of cake and invert onto serving plate. After cake is cooled completely, frost with Cream Cheese Frosting.

Cream Cheese Frosting: Mix together all ingredients except walnuts. Add small amount of skim milk if necessary for proper spreading consistency. Spread frosting on cake. Immediately sprinkle walnuts over top. (If you wait even a few minutes before sprinkling walnuts, frosting will be set and the nuts will slip off.)

Recipe courtesy of Janet M. Chiavetta, from *Eat, Drink and Be Healthy* (Fulcrum Publishing, 1995).

such as *Diet for a Small Planet* (the vegetarian text) and *Tassajara Cooking*, expanding their influence over the way Americans cooked and ate.

Support for organic foods meant rejection of "plastic" (standardized or highly processed) kinds. Brown rice, brown sugar, brown bread were hip. "Don't eat white; eat right and fight," was aimed at Wonder Bread as well as the White House.

Eating for Health

In 1961, Americans learned butter and cream contained saturated fat that raised their cholesterol levels, clogging arteries and causing heart disease. Ads for corn-oil margarine and skim milk were quick to suggest that families switch to food with polyunsaturated fat. Few paid much attention.

Vitamins were more interesting. Proponents thought vitamins worked miracles, particularly in megadoses. Vitamin A, for example, was said to wipe away acne while B vitamins corrected baldness. In 1966, Nobel Prize–winning chemist Linus Pauling campaigned to cure the common cold with Vitamin C. The FDA said supplements were not necessary for anyone eating a balanced diet, but in 1969 more than half of all Americans used vitamins and minerals, spending nearly half a billion dollars.

"The High Priestess of Nutrition" during the 1960s and 1970s was Adele Davis, whose books sold about ten million copies. She promoted the daily consumption of raw milk, eggs and cheese, whole grain cereals and organic foods, plus vitamin supplements. (Davis herself took six pills after every meal.) Controversy swirled around her. She was popular on talk shows but the bane of the medical community.

Health food stores, which had been tiny operations numbering no more than five hundred in 1965, blossomed by 1972 into three thousand or more food and vitamin boutiques, often with lunch counters. Consumer groups started five thousand to ten thousand nonprofit food co-ops in the 1970s to fight inflation and encourage organic farming. The co-ops carried counterculture foods such as whole grains, raw milk and herb tea. Estimated sales in 1975 topped $500 million, but hope that co-ops could sell food cheaply waned as it became clear they would not get quantity discounts available to supermarkets.

Made from rolled oats, granola is displayed here in numerous flavors. Selling organic foods, health food stores were typically small, independent operations thirty years ago. Today health food chain stores cater to a public concerned about the freshness and nutritional value of foods. This photo was taken at a health food store in Falls Church, Virginia, in 1973.

Ironically, about that time supermarkets ventured into the health food arena with fresh bean sprouts and tofu. In 1973, mainstream cereal makers launched versions of granola—nuts, dried fruits, grains and honey—far from Dr. Kellogg's unsweetened original. And in 1975, frozen yogurt debuted—an instant best-seller.

Never Too Thin

When not worrying about nutrition, many American women would fret about weight. In the 1960s, Carnaby Street miniskirts came into vogue. Women who followed the dictates of fashion magazines often tried to be shaped like supermodel Lesley Hornby, better known as Twiggy because of her lank, leggy look. It seemed true that "You can never be too rich or too thin," a quote attributed to both Babe Paley (the wife of CBS founder William Paley) and the Duchess of Windsor.

Style-conscious women downed gallons of Metrecal and similar "metered calorie" drinks—viscous liquids that contained only a few hundred calories, but were said to be as nourishing as an entire meal. Introduced to physicians in 1959, Metrecal quickly turned into a supermarket phenomenon—selling $350 million worth in 1961.

Two years later, Jean Nidetch and Albert Lippert founded Weight Watchers. A Queens, New York, housewife, Nidetch set up a support group to help herself lose weight. The group technique worked for her and dozens of others. Soon Weight Watchers programs were being held nationwide. In 1968, she went into the food business.

Diets abounded in magazines and books. Many were offbeat, some potentially dangerous in emphasizing a single food like grapefruit. Conventional wisdom said these were safe because a dieter would get too bored to stick them out for long. Sadly, dieting developed into an obsession for some—especially teenaged women. Everyday vocabulary soon extended to *anorexia*, for persons who fasted to the verge of starvation, and *bulimia*, for those who binged and purged, overeating, then making themselves vomit.

Additives or Negatives

By the late 1950s, chemists had produced nearly twenty-eight hundred food additives. Some reduced cost (artificial flavor, for example) and some improved nutrition (Vitamin C in fruit drinks). But most simply made food taste or look better longer.

Although processors argued that most additives were preserving standbys—sugar, salt, mustard and such—concern about chemicals led to the 1958 Food Additives Amendment to the 1938 Food and Drug Act. This established a list of seven hundred additives "generally regarded as safe" (the GRAS list) because long-term use showed them harmless. New additives would need FDA approval; those on the GRAS list could be used with no tests. Also exempt were about twelve hundred flavorings that passed tests prior to 1958. The 1960 Color Additive Amendment addressed two hundred or so colorings.

Consumers also got more explicit labeling. In 1974, the FDA ruled that labels must show ingredients in descending order of weight; in 1975, it ruled that food with nutritional claims must show to what degree nutrients met the Recommended Daily Allowance.

Health clubs and aerobics classes (like this one photographed in 1973) signed up members as people realized that fitness was more than avoiding excessive amounts of red meats. Sustained aerobics strengthens the heart muscle, making it less susceptible to disease.

COOKING UP WORLD HISTORY

Multicultural Recipes and Resources

~ Patricia C. Marden and Suzanne I. Barchers ~

Cover of a multicultural cookbook by Patricia C. Marden and Suzanne I. Barchers, published by Teacher Ideas Press in 1994. In the 1980s and 1990s, multicultural cooking hit its stride, with cuisines from all over the world becoming standard fare. (Cover courtesy of Teacher Ideas Press, a division of Libraries Unlimited, Inc., Englewood, Colorado.)

Chapter Ten
Wealthy and Wise (1980–Present)

*T*he high-flying glitterati of the 1980s—"If you've got it, flaunt it"—tended to become home-loving couch potatoes in the 1990s. During both decades, interest in fine foods escalated along with concern about calories, cholesterol, sodium and fat. Jogging and aerobics paved the way for personal trainers and vacations at fitness spas.

With a chorus of committees, the Food and Drug Administration and the Department of Agriculture began checking foods claiming to be "low" or "lite" or "lean." The resulting 1990 Nutrition Labeling and Education Act set up standard definitions of those words, and required that labels on processed food—including hot dogs as well as soft drinks—must clearly describe contents and nutrients by July 1994. Nutritional labeling for raw products was to be voluntary.

Meantime, the USDA gurus who had reshuffled food groups in 1956 to produce a pie chart that reduced the basic seven to a basic four—milk, meat, fruits and vegetables, breads and cereals—again scrambled the arrangement. The new pictograph was pyramidal to dramatize how much of each food must be eaten in a healthy diet. Grains and beans were in the large space at the base, fruits and vegetables in the next largest space, meat and dairy products in a smaller one, topped by fats and sweets in the tiny tip.

The Vegan Pyramid

When the U.S. Department of Agriculture devised its pyramidal food guide for Americans, it made no mention of vegetarians or vegans—pronounced vee-jans—who don't eat animal or dairy products. Dr. Arlene Spark, a professor at New York Medical College in Valhalla, New York, has solved the problem. In her special pyramid, she recommends that vegans balance their diets by the daily consumption of 6 to 11 servings of grains and starches such as potatoes (the pyramid's base), at least 3 servings of vegetables and 2 to 4 servings of fruit (second layer), and 2 to 4 servings of milk substitutes plus 2 to 3 servings of meat-fish substitutes like nuts and tofu (third layer). To supply the calcium, iron, riboflavin and vitamin B-12 that such a diet might lack, Dr. Spark tops her pyramid with daily use of 3 to 5 tablespoons of vegetable oil, and 1 tablespoon each of blackstrap molasses and brewer's yeast.

What's in Style

Abandoning the Continental gourmet track, the 1980s yuppies and dinks (young urban professionals and double-income/no-kids families) took up one food fad after another. Tex-Mex or Southwestern foods brought blue corn and jalapeño peppers into supermarkets, but were abandoned soon for Cajun cooking à la Paul Prudhomme. However, his emblematic blackened fish went out of style when explorers encountered the spicy grilled seafood of Southeast Asia.

New American Cooking was refined and defined many times, but beautiful presentation remained essential. Light and simple were catchwords. Portions were small, but presented artfully. Cakes contained just a few spoonfuls of flour; pasta was sauced with barely cooked vegetables; raw foods like Italian *carpaccio* (beef) or Japanese *sushi* (fish) came into vogue. Flower petals—nasturtium, rose, violet—brightened the *mesclun* salad mixture of cultivated and wild herbs and lettuces.

The increase and influence of the United States' growing Hispanic population is reflected in dietary trends; salsa now outsells ketchup as a condiment.

Foods that had been considered exotic a decade earlier became family standards—tortillas, pita bread, chick peas, even couscous. Sundried tomatoes were greeted with such glee and used so widely that they soon became old hat. Blue cornmeal replaced yellow and white types in breads and muffins. The grades of olive oil—virgin, extra virgin, first-press, second-press—were compared eagerly until upstaged by walnut oil. Devoted cooks created private-stock vinegar from wine and herbs or fruits, or experimented with balsamic vinegars.

Green peppercorns swept the market only to be ousted by red peppercorns (the fruit of the Brazilian pepper tree, not related to the pepper plant *piper nigrum*). Fresh herbs like basil, chives and dill turned up in supermarkets at last. Even exotics like Asian lemongrass appeared sometimes. Lucky the cook with a green thumb who could grow herbs in pots on windowsills and in an outdoor kitchen garden.

After years of reproducing ethnic foods faithfully, cooks felt brave enough to take liberties—topping pizza with beans, for example, or stuffing sausage casings with puréed fish and shrimp. By 1990, they were busily crossing one culinary line with another in international dishes like stir-fried fajitas or ravioli in wonton skins.

Braised Endive

8 heads Belgian endive, trimmed	2 tablespoons lemon juice
	2 tablespoons butter
1/2 cup chicken or beef stock	1 tablespoon sugar

Lay Belgian endive in one layer in a heavy skillet. Add chicken or beef stock, lemon juice, butter and sugar. Bring to a boil, reduce the heat, cover tightly and simmer for 30 minutes. Drain the endive, squeezing out excess liquid, and arrange them on a heated platter. Boil down the liquid left in the skillet to about 1/2 cup and pour it over the endive. Serves 4.

Picadillo

In Latin America and the Caribbean, picadillo may be topped with fried eggs, spooned over boiled rice or beans or used to fill tacos or bell peppers.

2 pounds ground beef	1/2 cup seedless raisins
2 tablespoons oil	1/2 cup pitted olives
1 large onion, chopped	1/2 teaspoon cinnamon
1 garlic clove, chopped	1/2 teaspoon cloves
2 cups chopped canned tomatoes	1/2 cup blanched slivered almonds
2 tablespoons chopped hot chilies	

Brown ground beef in oil until no pink shows. Stir in onion and garlic. Cook over low heat for a few minutes, then stir in tomatoes and chopped hot chilies, raisins, olives, cinnamon and cloves. Simmer uncovered, stirring often, for about 20 minutes. Taste for seasoning. Meanwhile, brown 1/2 cup blanched slivered almonds in 1 tablespoon oil. When the picadillo is thick and cooked through, add the almonds. Serves 4 to 6.

Aristocratic cuisines finally gave way to peasant styles in French *bistros* and Italian *trattorie*. American diner foods—Denver omelet, chicken-fried steak, butterscotch sundae—all became popular "retro" or comfort foods, reminding baby boomers of their childhoods. Even the most sophisticated of diners developed an obsession with chocolate desserts and candies. And in the mid-1990s, to everybody's (or nobody's) surprise, the 2-inch-thick beefsteak seemed to be making a comeback.

Spinach Frittata

Almost any vegetable can be used in the Italian version of the omelet: shredded zucchini, sliced mushrooms, florets of broccoli or cauliflower, even peeled and chopped tomatoes.

1 pound spinach	salt and pepper
2 tablespoons oil or butter	2 tablespoons grated
6 eggs	Parmesan cheese

Tear stems and blemishes from spinach. Wash the leaves, parboil them in lightly salted water for 2 minutes. Drain, run under cold water, and squeeze them dry. Chop spinach into shreds and sauté it for a few minutes in oil or butter in an ovenproof skillet set over low heat for a few minutes. Meanwhile, beat eggs lightly and season them with salt and pepper. Pour the eggs over the spinach, cover the skillet and cook for 4 or 5 minutes. When the top of the frittata begins to set, sprinkle it with Parmesan cheese and place the skillet under a hot broiler. When the cheese browns, slide the frittata onto a platter. Serve hot or cold, cut into wedges. Serves 4 to 6.

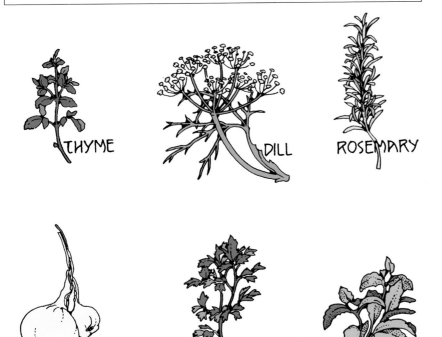

THYME   DILL   ROSEMARY

GARLIC   PARSLEY   MINT

Eat and Run

By 1990, fewer than 60 percent of families shared even one meal a day. Both parents had jobs in many cases; children had schedules of sports, club meetings and parties as well as school. The result was families that ate in shifts, putting microwaves to work defrosting frozen entrees or re-warming yesterday's dinner, then sitting in front of the TV to watch news or sitcoms while they ate.

Statistics showed that, on average, Americans nine years of age or older ate at a restaurant an average of four times a week and carried home or ordered delivery of four additional weekly meals. The operative "four food groups" became frozen, canned, delivered and take-out. When mom, dad and the children finally gathered around the table or television set for dinner, about a third of the families took advantage of convenient Shake 'n Bake or frozen lasagne. Two-thirds cooked from scratch, but less than half of these prepared gourmet-type dishes, now construed as food containing mushrooms or wine.

Cooks who served frozen pot pies during the week, of course, might become culinary whirlwinds on Saturday—baking cookies and cakes, molding terrines, churning ice cream. Making candy and preserving fruits turned out to be amazingly simple and rewarding recreations.

If guests were invited to dinner—on weekends or holidays, usually—food was presented with more éclat. There were silver and china and expanded menus with appetizers or first-course soups, salads, vegetable side dishes attending the main course and fancy desserts. Even the presumably casual brunch earned wine-soaked fruit and hot homemade biscuits.

The Ubiquitous Pasta

Everyone cooked pasta. The youngest members of the family could heat up canned or frozen varieties. It wasn't much more effort to boil one of the varied shapes—reputed to be four hundred or so—of dried pasta for saucing at home. Sauces, of course, came ready-made in jars or cans. Domestic pasta production topped four billion pounds by 1990 and showed no signs of slacking. (At that rate every man, woman and child in America must have downed 18 pounds per year!)

Most dried pasta was manufactured in the United States although imports increased from Asia as well as Europe. Fresh pasta, often colored and flavored by vegetables like carrots and beets, became a supermarket staple. Pasta machines, both manual and electric, simplified producing basic noodles and ravioli at home.

Paying More for Less

Many Americans, male as well as female, dieted (or tried to). Even if weight was no consideration, health was, as most adults came to realize that cholesterol could be their undoing. By the 1980s, nearly 20 percent of the money Americans spent for foods in supermarkets went for special low-calorie or diet varieties.

Publishers benefited in a big way from America's fat-phobia. By 1984, some three hundred diet books were in print according to historian Harvey Levenstein. Dr. Irwin Stillman's *Quick Weight Loss* book alone sold five million copies. As always, dieters exhibited ambivalence. For example, they would use sugar substitute in coffee they drank with a frosted Danish. Or they would "shape up, pig out"—dieting during the week so they could indulge on weekends.

Pasta Primavera

This dish fits the American idea of Italian cuisine and lighter eating combined. It was invented in New York at Le Cirque.

4 cups of fresh vegetables chosen from:
Snow peas, trimmed and cut in 1-inch pieces
Asparagus, 5 or 6 spears, cut in 1-inch pieces
Very small zucchini or summer squash, sliced thin or julienned
Small red bell pepper, seeded and julienned
Frozen or Fresh green peas
1 medium-size carrot, julienned
A small head of broccoli cut into florets

Sauce:
2 tablespoons olive oil
2 tablespoons butter
2 cloves garlic, finely chopped
1 cup sliced fresh mushrooms
1/3 cup finely chopped fresh parsley or basil
1 cup heavy cream
1/2 cup chicken stock

Pasta:
1 pound of thin pasta: fettucini, tagliatelli or vermicelli
3 tablespoons butter, softened

Topping:
1 cup freshly grated Parmesan cheese
1/2 cup toasted pine nuts

Parboil the vegetables separately, being sure they are still crisp, and set them aside. Prepare the sauce. In a large pan heat the olive oil and butter and sauté the garlic and mushrooms for a few minutes; add the parsley or basil. Add the vegetables and sauté for about 5 minutes, stirring frequently. Add the cream and chicken stock and heat. Meanwhile cook the pasta in a large pot of boiling water, until *al dente*. Drain, return to the pot and toss with the softened butter. Add the vegetables in the sauce, and the Parmesan cheese and toss with pine nuts. If the dish is too dry, you may add additional chicken broth, but the dish should not be liquid. Serves 4 to 6.

Low-Fat Lemon Bars

1-3/4 cups all-purpose flour	1-3/4 cups sugar
1/2 cup oatmeal (uncooked)	1/4 cup flour
1/2 cup powdered sugar	5 tablespoons fresh-squeezed
1/4 teaspoon salt	lemon juice
1/2 cup canola oil	powdered sugar
4 egg substitutes (1 cup)	

Preheat oven to 350°F. Combine first four ingredients in medium-size bowl. Gradually pour in cooking oil, stirring until well blended. (Small lumps will be present. Large lumps can be broken up with fingers.) Press flour mixture firmly into bottom of 9 x 13-inch nonstick pan. Bake for 15 minutes at 350°F. Meanwhile, in a medium-size bowl, combine egg substitutes, sugar, flour and lemon juice. Beat with a wire whisk. Pour over hot pastry. Bake an additional 20 minutes at 350°F. Remove from oven. Sprinkle with powdered sugar. Cut after cooled. Refrigerate until ready to serve.

Recipe courtesy of Janet M. Chiavetta, from *Eat, Drink and Be Healthy* (Fulcrum Publishing, 1995).

Chicken with Garlic

1 3- to 4-pound roasting	2 large heads of garlic
chicken	1 cup olive oil
salt and pepper	rosemary
parsley	celery rib
bay leaves	

Season the cavity of the chicken with salt and pepper, place a few parsley sprigs and a bay leaf inside and truss the bird. Separate the garlic cloves, but do not peel them. Drop the cloves into a heavy casserole just large enough to hold the chicken easily. Add olive oil and a bouquet garnish made by tying sprigs of parsley and rosemary and a bay leaf to a celery rib. Place the chicken in the casserole. Rub its skin with the oil, turning the bird to coat it evenly. Cover the casserole tightly and bake at 325°F for 1-1/2 hours. Serve the chicken and garlic from the casserole, accompanied by crusty bread; the garlic will be soft and easily squeezed out of its skins onto the bread. Its flavor will be mild. Serves 4.

The classiest places to get in shape were spas—never mind that they were laughingly called "fat farms." By the 1990s, more than 150 of them offered some version of the diet-exercise program innovated in America by Edmond and Deborah Szekely at Rancho La Puerta in Baja California. Michel Guérard's *cuisine minceur* also influenced menus that were already mostly vegetarian, with steamed, grilled or roasted foods flavored by herbs, spices and honey—never salt or sugar.

Food manufacturers continued searching for fatless fats and sugarless sugars while creating low-calorie versions of everything from bread to beer. Often the best they could do was to slice loaves ultra-thin and brew a drink with less alcohol. However, when Stouffers introduced Lean Cuisine, *The Washington Post* didn't complain about skimpy servings, but heralded the low-calorie dinners as the frozen food of the Jacuzzi set.

Although hog breeders produced a low-fat pig, turkey was already beginning to replace pork for bacon and sausages. In 1987, beef graded U.S. Good was renamed U.S. Select—making lean meat sound more palatable, no matter how flat its taste was. Chicken—most now marketed in parts—finally outsold beef in 1987 by 78 pounds per person to 73 pounds. (Cattle proponents pointed out that the boneless equivalents would have been 43 pounds of chicken meat to 69 pounds of beef.)

Just about all domestic cheeses had low-fat equivalents. Low-fat milk (1 or 2 percent butterfat) outsold regular (3.6 percent) after 1989; even skim milk (.5 percent) sales rose steadily.

Faux Foods

Fake, or *faux*, food was an ancient idea, resurrected with enthusiasm by dieters. Kosher dairy cooks and vegetarians around the world had long been turning grains, beans and nuts into artificial steaks and chops. Chicory and roasted grain were old substitutes for coffee. At the turn of the century, synthetic sweetening had found a ready market.

Then food scientists in the 1960s learned how to spin soybean fibers into protein analogs so manufacturers could approximate the texture of meat as well as its taste and color. Two decades later, dieters joined vegetarians as customers for *faux* hotdogs, breakfast sausages, hamburgers and cutlets. Annual sales quickly topped $65 million.

Inexpensive, cholesterol-free soybeans also became the base for ice-cream products. Milk protein and vegetable oil formed a low-priced stand-in for mozzarella cheese. Fish paste was colored, flavored and molded to create Japanese *surimi*, or artificial crab legs. Red-dyed dehydrated apples were the fruit in strawberry parfait. However, egg substitutes were 99 percent real egg—but only the whites. Flavoring and coloring simulated yolks.

Farm Fish

As concern about dieting increased, American consumption of seafood rose to about 15 pounds per person in 1992—half of which came from imports. With demand so far in excess of the supply of wild fish and shellfish, aquaculture became profitable.

By 1992, the tanks and ponds on America's thirty-four hundred or so fish farms produced a crop of about 850 million pounds. More than half (459 million pounds) of the catch was catfish, chiefly from Mississippi, Louisiana, Arkansas and Alabama. The rest of the finny crop included about 56 million pounds of trout (Idaho), nineteen million pounds of salmon (Washington and Maine) and close to 10 million pounds of tilapia (California). Louisianans farmed about 95 million pounds of crayfish.

Nutritional Roulette

Food scares erupted, then died. Advice about healthy diet changed so rapidly—fiber is good for you, no it isn't; salt is dangerous, not for everybody; coffee is dangerous, not really—that consumers often got angry as well as frustrated.

Cooks were warned that overdosing on nutritious food like carrots or on supplements like vitamin pills could have negative effects. Carrots turned the palms of consumers' hands and the soles of their feet yellow-orange, which hardly seemed a serious problem, but excess Vitamin A might lead to liver damage or hair loss.

Meringue Nests for Fruit

This is a recipe to make on a dry day in a dry week. Meringues can't stand humidity.

> 4 egg whites
> 1/8 teaspoon cream of tartar
> 1 teaspoon vanilla
> 1 cup sifted confectioners' sugar or superfine sugar
> sweetened raw or cooked fruit
> whipped cream (garnish)

To make the case, beat egg whites until foamy. Add cream of tartar and vanilla and continue beating until the whites begin to form soft peaks. Gradually beat in confectioners' sugar or superfine sugar. When the meringue stands in firm peaks, shape it into round or oval nests about 3 inches across on a piece of oil parchment paper. To form the nests, use a spoon or a pastry bag fitted with a plain or fancy tube. Bake the meringues for about 1 hour at 250°F. Let them cool in the oven for 10 minutes. To serve, fill the nests with sweetened raw or cooked fruit mixed, if desired, with whipped cream. Makes about 8.

Cajun cooking captured the imagination of the country with dishes spiced with peppers and fiery seasonings.

With all the hoopla, definitive answers seemed harder to get than ever. The 1989 Recommended Daily Allowance—the tenth since 1941—reflected the latest nutrition studies, and it adjusted, only slightly, the amounts of vitamins and minerals recommended by the RDA of 1980.

Fashions in Drinks

More than six hundred firms sold still or bubbly water bottled straight or with fruit flavorings at springs, wells or taps in countries around the world. Called "Designer Water," it was the drink of choice before and during meals. Like football players, figure skaters swigged it from the bottle. In 1993 Americans imbibed nearly three billion gallons of it.

The fashionable green Perrier bottle disappeared briefly in 1988 when a North Carolina laboratory found that the water contained traces of benzene (a possible carcinogen). After the problem was traced to filters and corrected, the bottle came back, but its new label read "natural mineral water." Although the water was naturally carbonated as previously claimed, its bubbles had to be removed for safe handling and replaced with CO_2 as it was bottled.

By 1990, Americans were drinking about 30 quarts of fruit juices and fruit drinks per person per year. Among these beverages "sports drinks" alone—with sodium and potassium to speed fluids through the body—constituted an $800 million business. Additionally, everybody downed 184 quarts annually of such carbonated soft drinks as colas and ginger ale.

Consumption of distilled spirits dropped to 8 quarts per person in 1990, while sales of wine and sweet wine coolers rose to more than 12 quarts. A glass of white wine was considered a stylish "cocktail." By then, about three-quarters of the wine sold was American made. California alone had at least six hundred wineries. Domestic vintages equaled many imports in quality and cost almost as much.

Beer was more popular than ever, although much of it was "light." Imports from Asia and

"White with fish and poultry, red with meat" was the old rule of thumb for selecting a dinner wine. It's not so simple anymore with so many vineyards and so many new and different varieties of wines.

Africa as well as Europe and Latin America swelled the drinker's choices to about four hundred brands. Both imports and mass-produced American beers were challenged by microbreweries that multiplied after federal laws regulating home brewing were relaxed in 1977. The foremost, Anchor Brewery of San Francisco, pumped out fifty-eight thousand barrels of beer in 1989, while Anheuser-Busch produced about

170,000 barrels daily, but they contributed variety including old-fashioned types of beer, ale, porter, stout and barleywine. By 1995 the microbreweries and brewpubs, which they spawned, were widespread enough to inspire a kind of Baedeker to guide Americans on a coast-to-coast sampling tour.

Glitzy Kitchens

The less time most families could spend—or needed to spend—in the kitchen, the more efficient its arrangement and equipment grew. The chintzy post-war kitchen was remodeled into an elegant working-dining space with materials that would prove practical as well as handsome: shiny plastic, stainless steel, polished wood and glowing marble. Cabinets had built-in lazy Susans, spice racks, flour bins and cutting boards. Refrigerators not only dispensed ice cubes and icy water, but were frost-free. Conventional ovens were self-cleaning. And by 1990, more than 75 percent of homes had microwave ovens.

Always intrigued by gadgets and mechanical marvels, American cooks now got an electric bread baker that turned out perfect loaves about 2 hours after the ingredients were poured into it. Coffee grinders crushed fresh beans, and ice cream makers guaranteed tasty results with no churning.

Super-Dooper Markets

Chain supermarkets grew to a median size of 32,000 square feet (about as big as a football field) with some 35,000 SKUs of which almost 20,000 units were food. Although nearly everyone in the family cooked, women still did three-quarters of the shopping.

Healthy food was an important part of the supermarket inventory. Alfalfa sprouts,

---

Plugged-In Cooks

Like their Victorian forebears, modern Americans pride themselves on their kitchen gadgets. By 1995, more than 90 percent owned microwave ovens and almost as many had blenders. Close to half had food processors. More specialized gear was owned—and used less. Bread machines, espresso machines and pasta machines all turned up in about 10 percent of the cooks' homes.

Salmon Teriyaki

1 to 1-1/2 pounds salmon fillets
2 tablespoons reduced-sodium soy sauce
1/4 cup Chablis wine
1/4 teaspoon paprika
1-1/2 teaspoons sugar

Wash salmon fillets and pat dry. Prepare marinade by combining soy sauce, wine, paprika and sugar. Place fillets in shallow container and pour marinade over. Marinate for 30 minutes at room temperature or 1 to 2 hours in refrigerator. Meanwhile, set oven control to broil. Spray broiler rack with vegetable cooking spray. Remove salmon from marinade and place on rack. Spoon 2 tablespoons of marinade over top of fish. Broil approximately 4 to 6 inches from heat, skin side down, for 8 to 10 minutes or until fish flakes easily with a fork. Place on platter and serve immediately. Garnish with lemon wedges. Serves 4.

Recipe courtesy of Janet M. Chiavetta, from *Eat, Drink and Be Healthy* (Fulcrum Publishing, 1995).

White Bean Salad

1/2 pound (1 cup) white kidney, marrow or navy beans	1/4 cup finely chopped scallions
lightly salted water	2 tablespoons chopped parsley
1/2 cup olive oil	1 7-ounce can tuna
2 tablespoons lemon juice	capers, parsley, lemon
salt and pepper	wedges (garnish)

Soak kidney, marrow or navy beans overnight; cook them in lightly salted water to cover for 2 hours or until tender. (Or drain a 16-ounce can of cannelloni beans and wash them in a colander.) Whisk together olive oil, lemon juice and a little salt and pepper. Stir in the beans, chopped scallions and parsley. Marinate the beans at room temperature for at least an hour. Taste for seasoning. Drain a 7-ounce can of tuna; divide it into 4 portions. To serve, spoon beans onto 4 salad plates. Place a portion of tuna atop each mound of beans. Garnish with capers, parsley and lemon wedges. Serves 4.

Gougère

An impressive, but remarkably easy hors d'oeuvre based on cream puff paste.

1 cup water	3 eggs, more if needed
8 tablespoons butter	1 cup grated Swiss cheese
1 cup flour	

In a heavy saucepan, bring water and butter to a boil. Reduce the heat and add flour all at once; stir vigorously until this mixture leaves the sides of the pan and forms a stiff ball. Remove the pan from the heat and quickly beat in 3 eggs, one at a time. The paste should be smooth and firm enough to hold its shape in a spoon. If necessary, add one or even two more eggs; start with one yolk alone—it may be enough. Beat in Swiss cheese. Using a spoon or a pastry bag fitted with a plain or fancy tube, shape the pastry into mounds 1-1/2 inches across and 2 inches apart on a buttered baking sheet. Bake at 400°F for 20 minutes or until puffed and brown. Makes about fifteen 3-inch puffs.

Banana Muffins

1 cup flour	2 mashed ripe bananas
1/2 cup sugar	1/4 cup flour
1 teaspoon cinnamon	2 tablespoons brown sugar
1 teaspoon baking powder	2 tablespoons whipped
1/2 cup skim milk	margarine
2 egg whites	

Combine flour, sugar, cinnamon, baking powder. Then stir in skim milk, egg whites and mashed bananas. Spoon batter into 8 muffin pan cups that have been coated with cooking spray. Sprinkle a mixture of 1/4 cup flour, 2 tablespoons brown sugar and 2 tablespoons whipped margarine over the batter. Bake at 400°F for 20 to 25 minutes or until browned. Cool the pan on a wire rack for 5 minutes before unmolding the muffins.

sunflower seeds, herbal teas and whole grains were *de rigeur*. Most markets found room for salad bars, similar to those in restaurants, with raw fruits and vegetables already peeled, cored and cut into bite-sized pieces. Nonetheless, some eight thousand health food stores flourished, with annual sales in excess of $4 billion. Besides organically grown vegetables and fruits, they proffered hormone-free poultry, nitrite-free bacon and preservative-free breads.

Convenience stores, often part of gas stations, aimed at the beer-and-cigarettes market by staying open around the clock. They also lured the once-weekly supermarket shopper who ran out of milk or bread. Where they encroached on business, supermarkets went on a 24-hour, 7-day schedule.

All kinds of markets got competition from discount warehouse stores that asked customers to pay membership fees before shopping. By the 1990s, more than 450 such stores were selling canned foods by the case and restaurant-sized containers of precooked frozen foods..

Counter to the supermarketing trend, gourmet stores that specialized in imported delicacies like glazed chestnuts and prosciutto thrived in big cities. Cheese stores and coffee stores profited from sophisticated cooks, willing to pay extra for superior quality. Everywhere, ethnic markets got new customers as shoppers searched for exotic ingredients. Farmers' markets proliferated, and greengrocers carried local, organically grown produce.

With increasing frequency, the quality of fruits and vegetables was a cook's chief criterion for picking a store. Supermarkets obliged and added to their selections. Tomatillos, enoki mushrooms, white eggplants and fennel were stocked regularly.

Cooking Schools and Books

The hundreds of local cooking schools popular in the early 1980s lost favor by the end of the decade. Hobbyists began to buy videocassettes showing their favorite teachers, or they watched them on TV as cable opened more channels and cooking classes were presented almost all day, every day.

Although *The Pleasures of Cooking* magazine succumbed in 1987, other food magazines thrived: *Gourmet*, *Food & Wine* and *Bon Appetit* (sold in 1993 to Condé Nast). Women's and shelter magazines, men's magazines, even nature and tourism magazines found ever more space for recipes.

Cookbooks spewed from presses at an amazing rate. In 1985 *Publishers Weekly* reported that 1,137 different new titles had appeared (compared to the measly forty-nine of 1960). And that figure did not include charity books written to raise money for an almost unimaginable variety of good causes ranging from churches to scout troops.

Today's Cook

In nearly four centuries, American cookery has become a distinctive cuisine with great diversity and complexity. Native ingredients and early English traditions blend with foods brought by later immigrants from every part of the globe. Different parts of the country boast a spectrum of regional borrowings and inventions.

For many Americans, the best foods are still the made-from-scratch dishes featuring fresh local ingredients. For others, the convenience of cooking with packaged products—whether canned, dried or frozen—proves irresistible. And many resist kitchen chores altogether, preferring to eat out at whatever restaurants their pocketbooks dictate: temples of *haute cuisine* (*nouvelle* or classic), ethnic specialists, family style eateries, steakhouses, cafeterias or fast-food emporiums.

The meat-and-potatoes menu seems to have survived the test of time, although watching cholesterol and salt intake has grown more widespread. And the American love affair with desserts and sweet snacks continues unabated—with aspartame making it possible to erase any feelings of guilt.

Like the country itself, America's cuisine is constantly changing. The rich bounty of America's lands and waters will always inspire innovation and a continuing flow of fine foods from amateur and professional cooks alike.

Taramasalata

The pink roe (tarama) of gray mullet is preserved with salt and available where Greek foods are sold. It makes a tangy dip for crudités.

6 thick slices homemade-type	juice of 2 lemons
white bread	1/4 cup grated onion
1/2 cup tarama	1 cup olive oil

Cut the crusts from bread and soak the slices briefly in water. Squeeze out the water, tearing the bread into bits. With a mortar and pestle or heavy bowl and spoon, gradually beat tarama into the bread, a spoonful at a time. Beat in the lemon juice and grated onion. When the mixture is smooth, transfer it to a large bowl. With a whisk or rotary beater, beat in about 1 cup olive oil—1 tablespoon at a time. After adding about 1/2 cup, the mixture should be creamy and smooth; whisking constantly, add more oil in a slow stream until the taramasalata is thick enough to hold its shape in a spoon. Taste for seasoning. Makes about 2 cups.

Cookbooks are big business—and big sellers. Thousands of new cookbooks, as well as books on diet and fitness, are published each year. This potpourri of food-oriented publications was photographed in 1981 by a photographer for *U.S. News and World Report*.

Bibliography

The American Heritage Cookbook and Illustrated History of American Eating and Dining. New York: American Heritage Publishing Co., 1964.

Anderson, Oscar E., Jr. *The Health of a Nation: Harvey W. Wiley and the Fight for Pure Food.* Chicago: University of Chicago Press, 1958.

Bailey Ronald H., *The Home Front: U.S.A., World War II.* Alexandria, VA: Time-Life Books, 1977.

Barbour, Philip L., ed. *The Complete Works of Captain John Smith.* vol. I. Published or the Institute of Early American History and Culture, Williamsburg, VA, by The University of North Carolina Press, Chapel Hill, NC, and London, 1986.

Beard, James. *Delights and Prejudices.* New York: Atheneum, 1964.

———. *Menus for Entertaining.* New York: Delacorte Press, 1965.

Beard, James, et al., eds. *The Cook's Catalogue.* New York: Harper & Row, 1975.

Beck, Simone, et al. *Mastering the Art of French Cooking.* New York: Pantheon Books, Knopf, 1961.

Belasco, Warren. *Appetite for Change.* New York: Pantheon Books, 1989.

Benet, Stephen Vincent. *Western Star.* New York: Farrar & Rinehart, 1943.

Bocuse, Paul. *Paul Bocuse's French Cooking.* Translated by Colette Rossant. Edited by Lorraine Davis. New York: Pantheon Books, 1977.

Bowen, Ezra, ed. *This Fabulous Century, Vols. I–IV.* New York: Time-Life Books, 1968–1969.

Bradford, William. *Historie Of Plymouth Plantation, 1620–1647.* Edited by Samuel Eliot Morison. New York: The Modern Library, 1952.

Bridge, Fred, and Jean F. Tibbetts. *The Well-Tooled Kitchen.* New York: William Morrow and Co., 1990.

Bryan, Mrs. Lettice. *The Kentucky Housewife.* Cincinnati: Shepard & Stearns, 1839.

California Heritage Continues. Junior League of Pasadena. New York: Doubleday, 1987.

Callahan, Carol. *Prairie Avenue Cookbook.* Carbondale, IL: Southern Illinois University Press, 1993.

Camp, Wendell H., et al. *The World in Your Garden.* Washington, DC: National Geographic Society, 1957.

Campbell, Hannah. *Why Did They Name It?* New York: Fleet Publishing Corp., 1964.

Cannon, Poppy. *The Can-Opener Cookbook.* New York: Thomas Y. Crowell Co., 1952.

Charvat, Frank J. *Fifty Years of Supermarketing.* New York: Macmillan & Co., 1961.

Claiborne, Craig. *Craig Claiborne's A Feast Made for Laughter.* Garden City, NY: Doubleday & Co., 1982.

————. *The New York Times Cook Book*. New York: Harper & Row, 1961.

Clark, Robert. *James Beard: A Biography*. New York: HarperCollins, 1993.

Colby, Jean Poindexter. *Plimouth Plantation Then and Now*. New York: Hastings House, 1970.

Cummings, Richard O. *The American and His Food*. Chicago: 1940.

Emerson, Everett H. *Captain John Smith*. New York: Twayne Publishers, 1993.

Feibleman, Peter A. *American Cooking: Creole and Acadian* from *Foods of the World*. New York: Time-Life Books, 1975.

Field, Michael. *All Manner of Food*. New York: Knopf, 1970.

Frederick, Christine. *Selling Mrs. Consumer*. New York: The Business Bourse, 1929.

Gallup, George H. *The Gallup Poll: Public Opinion, 1935–1971*. New York: Random House, 1972.

————. *The Gallup Poll: Public Opinion, 1972–1977*. Wilmington: Scholarly Resources, 1978.

Gourmet 50th Anniversary Issue. January 1991., vol. LI, no. 1. New York: Condé Nast Publications, 1991.

Guérard, Michel. *Michel Guérard's Cuisine for Home Cooks*. Translated and annotated by Judith Hill and Tina Ujlaki. New York: William Morrow and Co. 1976.

————. *Michel Guérard's Cuisine Minceur*. Translated by Narcisse Chamberlain with Fanny Brennan. New York: William Morrow and Co., 1986.

Hall, Carl W., Ph.D., and G. Malcolm Trout, Ph.D. *Milk Pasteurization*. Westport, CT: Avi Publishing Co., 1968.

Hamman, Mary, ed. *Picture Cook Book*. New York: Time Incorporated, 1958.

Hariot, Thomas. *Virginia: Four Personal Narratives (Thomas Hariot) A Briefe and True Report of The New Found Land of Virginia*. London: 1588.

Hess, John L., and Karen Hess. *The Taste of America*. Columbia: University of South Carolina Press, 1989.

Hibben, Sheila. *American Regional Cookery*. Boston: Little, Brown and Co., 1946.

Hillard, Sam Bowers. *Hog Meat & Hoecake: The Food Supply in the Old South from 1840 to 1880*. Carbondale: n.p., 1972.

Historical Statistics of the United States from Colonial Times to 1970. U.S. Department of Commerce, Bureau of the Census, U. S. Government Printing Office, 1975.

Hoffman, Mark S., ed. *The World Almanac and Book of Facts*. New York: Pharos Books, 1993.

Hooker, Richard J. *Food and Drink in America: A History*. Indianapolis/New York: Bobbs-Merrill Co., 1981.

Jones, Evan. *American Food: The Gastronomic Story*. New York: Vintage Books, 1981.

———— *Epicurean Delight: The Life and Times of James Beard*. New York: Knopf, 1990.

California Heritage Continues. Junior League of Pasadena, New York: Doubleday, 1987.

Langdon, Philip. *Orange Roofs, Golden Arches*. New York: Knopf, 1986.

Lebhar, Godfrey M. *Chain Stores in America*. New York: Chain Store Publishing, 1963.

Levenstein, Harvey. *Paradox of Plenty*. New York: Oxford University Press, 1993.

————. *Revolution at the Table*. New York: Oxford University Press, 1988.

Lifshey, Earl. *The Housewares Story*. Chicago: National Housewares Manufacturers Association, 1973.

Lingeman, Richard L. *Don't You Know There's a War On?/The American Home Front 1941–1945.* New York: G. P. Putnam's Sons, 1970.

Luchetti, Cathy. *Home on the Range.* New York: Villard Books, 1993.

Lynes, Russell. *The Domesticated Americans.* New York: Harper & Row, 1963.

Margolius, Sidney. *Health Food Facts and Fakes.* New York: Walker, 1973.

Mariani, John. *America Eats Out.* New York: William Morrow and Co., 1991.

———. *The Dictionary of American Food & Drink.* New Haven and New York: Ticknor & Fields, 1983.

Mayer, Jean, and Jean P. Goldberg. *Dr. Jean Mayer's Diet & Nutrition Guide.* New York: Pharos Books, 1990.

Meat for the Multitudes, vols. 1 and 2. Chicago: The National Provisioner, 1981.

Montagne, Prosper. *Larousse Gastronomique.* Edited by Carlotte Turgeon and Nina Froud. New York: Crown Publishers, 1961.

Paddleford, Clementine. *New York Public Library Book of Twentieth Century Quotations: How America Eats.* New York: Charles Scribner's Sons, 1960.

Parloa, Maria. *Home Economics: A Practical Guide in Every Branch of Housekeeping.* New York: The Century Co., 1910.

Penner, Lucille Recht. *The Colonial Cookbook.* New York: Hastings House, 1976.

Piercy, Caroline B. *The Shaker Cook Book: Not by Bread Alone.* New York: Crown Publishers, 1953.

Recommended Dietary Allowances, 10th ed. National Research Council. Washington, DC: National Academy Press, 1989.

Riepma, S. F. *The Story of Margarine.* Washington, D.C.: Public Affairs Press, 1970.

Root, Waverly. *Food.* New York: Simon and Schuster, 1980.

Root, Waverly, and Richard de Rochemont. *Eating in America.* New York: William Morrow and Co., 1976.

Selitzer, Ralph. *The Dairy Industry in America.* New York: Books for Industry, 1976.

Shapiro, Laura. *Perfection Salad.* New York: Farrar, Straus and Giroux, 1986.

Sokolov, Raymond. *Why We Eat What We Eat.* New York: Summit Books, 1991.

Spencer, Robert F., and Jesse D. Jennings. *The Native Americans.* New York: Harper & Row, 1965.

Statistical Abstract of the United States, 1982–1983. U.S. Department of Commerce, Economics and Statistics Administration, Bureau of the Census, U. S. Government Printing Office, 1983.

Stern, Jane and Michael. *American Gourmet.* New York: Knopf, 1984.

———. *Square Meals.* New York: Knopf, 1984.

The Story of a Pantry Shelf. Butterick Publishing Co., New York, 1925.

Strasser, Susan. *Never Done.* New York: Pantheon, 1982.

Szekely, Deborah. *Vegetarian Spa Cuisine from Rancho La Puerta and Deborah Szekely.* Edited by Roberta Ridgely. Escondido, CA: Rancho La Puerta, 1990.

Tannahill, Reay. *Food in History.* New York: Crown Publishers, 1988.

Turner, James. *The Chemical Feast.* New York: Grossman, 1970.

This Fabulous Century, vols. I–IV. New York: Time-Life Books, 1968–1969.

Trager, James. *The Enriched, Fortified, Concentrated, Country-Fresh, Lip-Smacking, International, Unex-purgated Foodbook*. New York: Grossman Publishers, 1970.

Visser, Margaret. *Much Depends on Dinner*. New York: Collier Books, Macmillan Publishing Co., 1986.

————. *The Rituals of Dinner*. New York: Grove Weidenfeld, 1991.

Waldman, Carl. *Atlas of the North American Indian*. New York: Facts on File Publications, 1985.

————. *Encyclopedia of Native American Tribes*. New York: Facts on File Publications, 1988.

Weatherford, Jack. *Indian Givers*. New York: Crown Publishers, 1988.

Whelan, Elizabeth M., and Frederick J. Stare. *Panic in the Pantry*. New York: Atheneum, 1977.

Wiley, Harvey. *Foods and Their Adulteration*. Philadelphia: Blakiston's & Sons, 1911.

Wyman, Carolyn. *I'm A Spam Fan*. Stamford, CT: Longmeadow Press, 1992.

Sources

Illustrations in this book come from various divisions within the Library of Congress. The Prints and Photographs Division (P&P) holds, among its millions of items, the following discrete collections, cites to which will be found on these pages: Historic American Buildings Survey (HABS); the Poster Collection (Pos.); American Cartoons (AMC); the Cabinet of American Illustration (CAI); Popular Graphic Arts (PGA); Fine Prints (FP); the New York World-Telegram & Sun Collection (NYWT&S); Farm Security Administration photos (FSA); and materials shelved in "Lots" (LOT). Illustrations also were drawn from the Rare Book and Special Collections Division (RBD); the Manuscript Division (MSS); the American Folklife Center (AFC); and the General Collections (Gen.).

Those who wish to order reproductions of illustrations in this book should contact the Library's Photoduplication Service and cite the Library of Congress negative numbers, or item call numbers provided below. Please note: Negative numbers begin with the following prefixes: BR8- (American Folklife Center negative), LC-MS- (Manuscript Division negative), LC-USZ62-, LC-USZ9-, LC-USZC2- (color), LC-USZC4- (color), LC-D4-, LC-F8, LC-USE-, LC-LSF-, LC-U9-, and LC-LSW. All other numbers are call numbers for the books or other materials from which the illustration was taken (when these numbers are unavailable, the division housing the item is indicated). When multiple images appear on a page, negative numbers (or other identifying information) will be given in the order the images are arranged, left to right, top to bottom.

Front matter: (opp. title page) PGA-B-Prang ("Currants"); (CIP page) BR8-LE23-15; (vi) LC-USZ62-20486; (vii) LC-USZC4-1206; (x) LC-USZ62-53339.

Introduction: (xi) LC-USZ9-274-2; (xii) LC-USZ62-1315.

Chapter One: (1) LC-USZ62-17899; (3) LC-USZ62-33923, LC-USZ62-37896; (4) LC-USZ62-15195; (5) LC-USZ62-33923; (6)TX703 .B7 [RBD], SB97. P24 (1656) p. 517 (RBD); (8) LC-USZ62-23635.

Chapter Two: (9) LC-USZ62-7782; (10) LC-USZ62-113520, LC-USZ62-144698, LC-USZ62-5370; (11) LC-USZ62-21251; (12) HABS Del-51 Sheet 3 [P&P]; (13) LC-USZ62-16771, LC-USZ62-38645; (14) CAI-B-Schmidt-1 [P&P], LC-MS-27748-180; (15) LC-USZC4-674 (color) or LC-USZ62-12431(b/w), LC-USZ62-31835; (16) LC-USZ62-2055, TX 717 .H515 1857 [RBD]; (17) HABS MD 8-Earl 2A-4 [P&P]; (18) LC-USZ62-20979, LC-USZ62-2750, HABS Del 2-NAMA 1-2 [P&P]; (19) TX 717 .H515 1857 [RBD], LC-USZ62-34041; (20) TX 717 .H515 1857 [RBD]; (21) F273 .565 [RBC]; (22) AP2 .A2U6 [RBD].

Chapter Three: (23) LC-USZ62-54204; (24) LC-USZC2-248, LC-USZ62-47192; (25) LC-USZ62-20480, LC-USZC2-171; (26) LOT 6423-F [P&P]; (27)LC-USZ62-1083; (28) LC-USZC4-4403 (color), LC-USZC4-1259;

(29) LC-USZ62-12436, TX715 .H829 [Gen.]; (30) LC-USZ62-11780; (31) LOT 2639 [P&P], LC-USZ62-11767; (32) TX715 .H829 [Gen.] [cookbook page], LC-USZC4-3611 [mincemeat ad], CAI-A-Frost-35 [P&P, chestnuts], LC-USZC2-250 [flavoring ad]; (34) LC-USZ62-18; (36) CAI-C-Stephens-29 [P&P], LC-USZC4-1154 (color) or LC-USZ62-32390 (b/w) [food chopper], LC-USZC4-775 (color) or LC-USZ62-2589 (b/w) [home washing machine]; (37) LC-USZC2-169, LC-USZC4-674; (38) LC-USZ62-479, AP2 .L135 (Ladies' Home Journal) [Gen]; (39) LC-USZ62-33606.

Chapter Four: (40) LC-USZC2-418 (color) or LC-USZ62-54590 (b/w); (42) LC-USZ62-61199, LC-USZ62-54595; (43) LC-USZ62-32479; (44) LC-USZ62-11379, LC-USZ62-25665; (45) TX1 .C8 (Cooking Club Magazine, Mar. 1902 [Gen.], AP2 .H32 (Harper's Weekly, 1916) [Gen.]; (46) LC-D423-601; (47) LC-USZ62-98431, LC-USZ62-94241; (48) FP (Glavanis) [P&P], LC-USZ62-4553; (49) TX791 .W3 [Gen.], LC-USZ62-48289; (50) LC-USZ62-105451; (51) CAI-B-Fogarty, (Thomas)-21 [P&P]; (52) LC-USZC2-423 (color) or LC-USZ62-54959 (b/w), TX715 .H678 [Gen.].

Chapter Five: (53) AMC (Charles Lewis Bartholomew)[P&P]; (54) LOT 12353-10 [P&P]; (56) LOT 12353-10 [P&P]; (57) LOT 12353-10 [P&P]; (58) NA7100 .B45 (Better Homes & Gardens, 1920s) [Gen], AP2 .L58 (Literary Digest, 1920s [Gen]; (59) LC-USZ62-42412, Gen. (Good Housekeeping, July 1927); (60) LC-USZ62-33705; (61) LOT 4777-2 [P&P], LC-USZ62-110367, LC-F8-18018; (62) LOT 12353-10 [P&P]; (63) LC-D420-2718; (64) LOT 12353-10 [P&P].

Chapter Six: (65) LC-USF33-2196-M3, LC-USF342-8093-A; (66) LC-USF34-2911-D; (67) LOT 12353-10 [P&P]; (68) LC-USF34-55551-D, LC-USF33-20523-M1; (70) LC-USF35-268 (color slide-similar view), LC-USF33-12209-M4; (71) LC-USF34-14364-D; (73) LC-USF34-60122D; (74) LC-USF351-358; (75) FP (Howard Cook) [P&P].

Chapter Seven: (76) LC-USE-6-D-10147; (78) LC-USZC4-1606; (79) LC-USW361-644; (83) LC-USE6-D-9443; (85) LC-USZ62-32893.

Chapter Eight: (88) Gen. (Look, 1956); (89) Gen. (Good Housekeeping, Nov. 1956, p. 125); (90) NYWT&S [P&P]; (91) NYWT&S [P&P]; (92) Gen. (Life, 5/17/54); (93) Gen. (Look, 6/26/56); (96) Gen. (Look, 5/15/56, p. 49), Gen. (Look, 6/26/56, p. 44); (97) Gen. (Life, 4/3/54); (99) NYWT&S [P&P].

Chapter Nine: (101) LC-USZC2-50; (102) LC-U9-13455; (103) LC-U9-18593; (104) LC-U9-14039-31; (105) AFC—all 3 images; (107) LC-U9-13453; (108) AFC—all 3 images; (110) LC-U9-28238; (111) LC-U9-34590, LC-U9-40441-17; (112) LC-U9-36006, LC-U9-23057-34; (114) LC-U9-27486-15A; (115) LC-U9-36868B-13.

Chapter Ten: (116) TX725.A1 M347 1994; (118) P&P; (123) P&P; (126) LC-U9-40449-24.

Index

"Syrupping off" days, 68 (photo)
Szekely, Edmond and Deborah: diet-exercise program by, 121
Tableware, 96
  early, 8, 19
Taffy pulls, 35
Taggart Baking Company, Wonder Bread and, 56
Taramasalata, recipe for, 126
Tassajara Cooking, 113
Tavernier, Jules: drawing by, 24
Taxco Market, 75 (illustration)
Tea parties, 11, 25–27, 41
Television
  cooking shows on, 99
  impact of, 96
Temperance, 21–22, 61
Thatcher, Harvey D., 50
Thomas, H.: lithograph by, 28
Time-Life Books, cookbooks by, 110
Toasters, 42 (photo), 45, 55, 98
Toastmaster, toasters by, 55
"Toll House Cookies," 69
Tomatoes, xii, 17, 64
Tomato catsup, advertisement for, 24
Tower, Jeremiah, 106
Trading stamps, 98–99, 112
Traite General des Pesches (de Monceau), 3, 5
Trash compactors, 109
Treatise on Domestic Economy (Beecher), 20
Trenchard: woodcut by, 22
Trenchers, 8
Triscuit crackers, 35
Troisgros, Jean and Pierre, 105
Tugwell, Rexford Guy, 74–75
Tuna Fish Pâté, recipe for, 94
Tuna Helper, 102
Tupperware, 97
Turkey, 3, 4, 5, 31, 51 (illustration), 107, 121
TV dinners, 94
  advertisement for, 96
  cartoon about, 101
Twinkies, 72

Udico, can opener by, 97
Underwood's Red Devil Ham Spread, 29
United States Department of Agriculture
  food group classifications by, 116, 117
  instructors from, 56 (photo)
  labeling and, 117
  pressure canners and, 98
United States Food Administration (USFA), 51
  poster by, 52

Upside Down Cake, recipe for, 55
USDA. *See* United States Department of Agriculture
USFA. *See* United States Food Administration
U.S. News and World Report, 127
Utensils, 96
  early, 8, 19

Vachon, John: photo by, 73
Vallejo, Mariano: wine and, 94
Veal, 31, 67
Vegan Pyramid, 117
Vegetarians, faux foods and, 121
Vergé, Roger, 105
Vichyssoise, recipe for, 42
Victory gardens, 82
Victory lunch, 76 (photo)
Virginia Housewife, The (Randolph), 20
Vischer, Alfred, Jr., 98
Vitamins, 51, 63, 113, 114, 115
  health and, 64
  overdosing on, 123
  popularity of, 73–74
Vodka, 91, 107

Wait, Pearl B.: Jell-O and, 34
Wakefield, Ruth: Toll House Cookies and, 69
Waldorf Salad, recipe for, 26
War Gardens, 40 (drawing)
Warhol, Andy, 102
Waring, Fred, 73
Warner, Ezra J.: canning and, 17
Wartime Food Demonstrator, 83 (photo)
War Times Recipes, illustration from, 52
Washburn Crosby Company, 55
Washing machine, advertisement for, 36
Washington Market, 24 (painting)
Washington Post, The: on Lean Cuisine, 121
Waters, Alice, 106
Waxman, Jonathan, 106
"Wear-Ever," 46
Weight Watchers, 114
West, cooking in, 15–16
Westinghouse
  patio cart by, 91 (photo)
  toaster-stove by, 45
Whirlpool, trash compactor by, 109
Whiskey, 62, 81, 91
White, E. B.: on cooking, 66
White Bean Salad, recipe for, 124
Whiting Bros.: photo by, 47
Whitney, Eli, 12
Wiley, Harvey Washington, 74, 75

List of Recipes

Books in the Library of Congress Classics series
from Fulcrum Publishing:

America's Botanical Beauty by James L. Reveal

Americans on the Move by Russell Bourne

The Book in America by Richard W. Clement

Celebration of American Food by Gerry Schremp

The First Americans by William H. Goetzmann

Invention in America by Russell Bourne

The Library of Congress by Carol Highsmith and Ted Landphair

Mapping the Civil War by Christopher Nelson

Prints of the West by Ron Tyler

In addition:

Jefferson the Man by Robert C. Baron

Civil War Maps from the Library of Congress collection

Celebration of American Food

The text type is Berkeley Book and Eras, both by Adobe Systems, Incorporated.
All images were provided by the Library of Congress.
Book composed by Fulcrum Publishing, utilizing Macintosh systems and Adobe PageMaker 6.0.
Color separations by Sung In Printing Company, Seoul, Korea, at 200 line screen.
Text paper is 150 gsm matte art paper, printed utilizing four-color process.
Endsheets are 150 gsm Woodfree, printed PMS 485.
Printed and bound by Sung In Printing Company, Seoul, Korea, utilizing Cho Yang cloth, smythe-sewn
on three millimeter binder's board, with headbands and footbands, stamped in gold foil.